Digital Humanism

Hannes Werthner

Digital Humanism

On Digitalization and Artificial Intelligence

 Springer

Hannes Werthner
Institute of Information Systems Engineering
Technical University of Vienna
Vienna, Austria

ISBN 978-3-031-86904-4   ISBN 978-3-031-86905-1   (eBook)
https://doi.org/10.1007/978-3-031-86905-1

The original submitted manuscript has been translated into English. The translation was done using artificial intelligence. A subsequent revision was performed by the author(s) to further refine the work and to ensure that the translation is appropriate concerning content and scientific correctness. It may, however, read stylistically different from a conventional translation.

Translation from the German language edition: "Digital Humanism - Über Digitalisierung und künstliche Intelligenz" by Hannes Werthner, © 2024, Picus Verlag, Vienna, Austria. All Rights Reserved.

© The Editor(s) (if applicable) and The Author(s), under exclusive license to Springer Nature Switzerland AG 2025

This work is subject to copyright. All rights are solely and exclusively licensed by the Publisher, whether the whole or part of the material is concerned, specifically the rights of reprinting, reuse of illustrations, recitation, broadcasting, reproduction on microfilms or in any other physical way, and transmission or information storage and retrieval, electronic adaptation, computer software, or by similar or dissimilar methodology now known or hereafter developed.
The use of general descriptive names, registered names, trademarks, service marks, etc. in this publication does not imply, even in the absence of a specific statement, that such names are exempt from the relevant protective laws and regulations and therefore free for general use.
The publisher, the authors and the editors are safe to assume that the advice and information in this book are believed to be true and accurate at the date of publication. Neither the publisher nor the authors or the editors give a warranty, expressed or implied, with respect to the material contained herein or for any errors or omissions that may have been made. The publisher remains neutral with regard to jurisdictional claims in published maps and institutional affiliations.

This Springer imprint is published by the registered company Springer Nature Switzerland AG
The registered company address is: Gewerbestrasse 11, 6330 Cham, Switzerland

If disposing of this product, please recycle the paper.

Preface

Information technology is changing our society and our world, from the individual level to the current geopolitical disputes and power games. From an ontological perspective, it influences how we perceive the world and how we think about it. This change, enabled by digitalization,[1] which took place in a short period of just about 80 years and continues (and will not end), is particularly evident in the current developments in the field of artificial intelligence. This book describes this rather complex, not only technical development and some of its most important features. In particular, the dynamics of this process are highlighted, and some of the developments are critically reflected upon. At the beginning, I give a brief introduction to artificial intelligence, and then I discuss informatics as the fundamental science behind this development. This is followed by a description of the Web, its dynamics, and its rather specific laws. Like every technology in the history of mankind, this one also has both positive and negative effects on us, our lives, and our society. Some of these problems are discussed, and our positive response to them is described: digital humanism. This approach explains and analyzes the complex interplay of technology and humans, and it also tries to influence the development—for a better sustainable society and a better life respecting human rights. It is a holistic and proactive approach that focuses on the integration of technical and social innovation. At the end, I will introduce our digital humanism initiative and address the challenges it faces. The task of digital humanism seems simple and yet is very complicated.

This book is the English and slightly expanded version of Werthner (2025), which was published in early 2025. I add an important note, especially in the

---

[1] Note the difference between digitization and digitalization (often also used synonymously): Digitization is about data conversion (analog to digital), whereas digitalization is about process transformation using digital tools and technologies. Digitalization builds on digitization, but both are key elements of the digital transformation, which transforms not only processes but also societal structures and interactions. Since I refer to the entire process of transformation in this book, I will use the term digitalization.

v

context of this book: the translation was significantly supported and facilitated by the use of AI tools, but not totally automated.[2] Human intelligence is needed.

It is not a scientific book in the strict sense; it is one of science communication. It describes and interprets, sometimes it also evaluates, from my subjective point of view. The book is aimed at a broad readership and assumes no specific prior knowledge, just an interest in the subject. However, it is sometimes necessarily also a bit technical, but I have tried to remain understandable and to maintain a big picture. Digital humanism as well as this publication deals with changes on a technical but also on a social, political, and economic level. Their description and analysis require not only informatics but also other disciplines such as philosophy, economics, history, sociology, law, or political science. This breadth makes it nearly impossible to ensure the treatment of the topic is seamless and error-free. I hope not to have fallen into the trap of "interdisciplinary," knowing nothing or only trivial things about many things.

Finally, this book will never be "finished" and written to the end, and this is due to the rapid technical and political-regulatory development, which is especially the case here. During the translation work, it became clear that a lot has changed in just 6 months, and I have tried to incorporate this as far as possible—but the core statements and observations have been confirmed. This concerns not only the "technical" side with its rapid development with new tools and greater performance capabilities and new companies but also the political and regulatory side. This applies in particular to the USA, where it is not clear where the journey will take us after the political change in January 2025 with its new administration. This will affect the entire world due to the importance of the USA. It is to be expected (or feared) that there will be setbacks in the area of regulation and "social control,"[3] particularly because representatives of the large US IT companies will now be increasingly heard or will make efforts to be heard. However, this could also apply to Europe, where, due to changes in the political majority, regulatory activities could be slowed down or even reversed with the argument of competitiveness.

In that sense, this material will always be incomplete.[4]

Vienna, Austria   Hannes Werthner

---

[2] DeepL (from the German company DeepL) and Google Translate.

[3] However, there are also voices that advise caution against a hasty pessimistic assessment (see Rotenberg, M: "After the US Elections: The Future of AI Policy and Digital Humanism": Digital Humanism lecture, Nov 26, 2024; https://dighum.org/dighum-lectures/marc-rotenberg-after-the-us-elections-the-future-of-ai-policy-and-digital-humanism-2024-11-26/).

[4] Thanks to my colleague Georg Gottlob (TU Wien), who often begins his lectures with this note.

Acknowledgments

This text is the English translation of a German book based on a Vienna Lecture I gave in Vienna in March 2024.[1] I was happy to accept the invitation of the organizer, the Vienna City Library, a "department" of the Vienna City Administration, to turn my lecture into a book (in German). For this and for the support, I thank the Vienna City Library and its director, Anita Eichinger, and her team (especially Silvia Wahrstätter for the graphics and Caro Schenk for supervising the book project). I would also like to thank Springer Verlag, in particular Ralf Gerstner, who offered to publish the book in English and then supported me with the translation and did a very good job of editing.

The original request to write a book was not only an opportunity but also an invitation to sit down after 5 years of digital humanism, after the publication of two very successful anthologies on the subject (also published by Springer), and to comprehensively describe this approach for a fairer (digital) world as one of its main representatives. This also served to explain the technical economic background and to embed this approach in the context of society as a whole.

But the story of the book actually begins much earlier, during my time as a university assistant at the University of Vienna. Back then, in the 1980s, I held seminars on "women and Informatics" as well as "society and Informatics" together with my colleague and current dean of the Faculty of Informatics at TU Wien, Gerti Kappel. These seminars were very well received by the students. Unfortunately, the problems discussed there are still with us today, and it is no coincidence that Gerti Kappel is a strong supporter of digital humanism—thank you!

The topic of the interaction between informatics and society returned years later when, in my role as dean of the Faculty of Informatics at TU Wien, in 2016 I have set up an International Advisory Board (IAB) to provide content-related support, advice, and evaluation. Over time, our meetings went far beyond informatics; they

---

[1] The Vienna lecture (Wiener Vorlesung) is a public lecture series organized by the city of Vienna since 1987. It features high-profile talks from experts in science, culture, and politics on current topics, aiming to foster societal dialogue. The events are free and open to all, with the goal of making knowledge accessible and encouraging discussions.

revolved around its role as a discipline and that of the university as an institution in society. For these discussions and intellectual challenges, I am greatly indebted to Hans Akkermans, Carlo Ghezzi, Edward Lee, Nadia Magnenat-Thalmann, and Moshe Vardi, the members of the IAB. They are still actively involved in our initiative.

These discussions led to the Vienna Workshop on digital humanism and, as a result, the Vienna Manifesto. Here, my thanks go to the Faculty of Informatics and also to Michael Stampfer (WWTF-Vienna Science and Technology Fund) for their support. Looking back, the workshop was the "organizational" start of the initiative, not formally, but in the form of a more or less loose group of people. I would especially like to thank Stefan Woltran, Peter Knees, Julia Neidhardt, and Walter Palmetshofer from the Faculty of Informatics at TU Wien and Erich Prem from the now formally founded Digital Humanism Association. Activities such as our lecture series, conferences, and summer schools would not exist without them. Another strand of activities that began after the workshop is the Digital Humanism Fellowship Program at the IWM, which is funded by the BMK (Austrian Federal Ministry Climate Action, Environment, Energy, Mobility, Innovation, and Technology). Here I would like to thank Ludger Hagedorn (IWM-Institut für die Wissenschaft vom Menschen) and Michael Wiesmüller (BMK).

Another almost logical consequence[2] was the contact with the philosopher Julian Nida-Rümelin and the cultural scientist Nathalie Weidenfeld, who described and defined the philosophical foundations of our now common approach in their German standard work on digital humanism (Nida-Rümelin & Weidenfeld, 2018). Our collaboration shows that philosophy, cultural studies, and computer science do have a lot in common.

But especially, I thank the co-editors and authors of our books *Perspectives on Digital Humanism* (Werthner et al., 2022b) and *Introduction to Digital Humanism* (Werthner et al., 2024), the members of our international Steering Committee, as well as the organizers of our many workshops and conferences. They represent the intellectual core of digital humanism, so to speak. In alphabetical order—and in partial overlap with the already-mentioned persons—these are Hans Akkermans, Ricardo Baeza-Yates, Amel Bennaceur, Anna Bon, Robin Burke, Brian Butler, Cansu Canca, Michael Caspersen, Cristiano Codagnone, Claude Draude, Anita Eichinger, Usama Fayyad, Alfonso Fuggetta, Walter Gehr, Carlo Ghezzi, Misha Glenny, Jaap Gordijn, Lynda Hardman, Nathalie Hauk, Manfred Hauswirth, Clemens Heitzinger, Christoph Thun-Hohenstein, Walter Hötzendorfer, Paola Inverardi, Matthias Kettemann, Peter Knees, Sabine Koeszegi, Jeff Kramer, Brigitte Krenn, Jim Larus, Edward Lee, Martina Lindorfer, Nadia Magnenat-Thalmann, Ciaran Martin, Sunimal Mendis, George Metakides, Martin Müller, Luke Munn, Leena Murgai, Irina Nalis, Enrico Nardelli, Julia Neidhardt, Wolfgang Nejdl, Clara Neppel, Julian Nida-Rümelin, Helga Nowotny, Bashar Nuseibeh, Hubert Österle, Geoffrey Parker, Niki Popper, Katharina Prager, Erich Prem, Alexander Pretschner,

---

[2] In retrospect, many things seem simple and logical.

Martin Rauchbauer, Elissa Redmiles, Wolfgang Renner, Marc Rotenberg, Stuart Russell, Francis Saa-Dittoh, Daniel Samaan, Viola Schiaffonati, Ute Schmid, Sebastian Schrittwieser, Johanna Seibt, Helen Sharp, Patricia Shaw, Joseph Sifakis, Michael Stampfer, Allison Stanger, Klaus Staudacher, Oliviero Stock, Guglielmo Tamburrini, Paul Timmers, Christoph Thun-Hohenstein, Moshe Vardi, Nathalie Weidenfeld, Edgar Weippl, Christiane Wendehorst, Dorothea Winter, Susan Winter, Stefan Woltran, Sally Wyatt, and George Zarkadakis.

As I compile this list, I realize that it is almost impossible to name all those involved in our many activities, and I am sure I have forgotten some. They may not be angry with me. Digital humanism, as well as this book, would not have been created and possible without all the mentioned and unmentioned. Thanks to all—actually, this is their book.

Contents

1	**Introduction**..	1
	Briefly: The Information Society	3
2	**Artificial Intelligence**	9
	But: There Is No Free Lunch	11
	AI: A Discussion Between Dystopia and Utopia	13
	What Is AI?...	15
	The Two Methods of AI	17
	And Now LLM (Large Language Model)	23
	Anthropomorphism: AI Like a Human?........................	29
	Are We Demanding Too Much of the Machine?	32
	AI: A Preliminary Balance	32
3	**Informatics**...	39
	The Nature of Informatics....................................	39
	Brief History of Informatics	42
4	**The Web**...	55
	Economic Impact	61
	Efficiency Versus Resilience...................................	63
	Digitalization: Cause or Solution	65
5	**Platforms**	69
	Platform as the Dominant Organizational Form in the Digital Age?...	73
	Platforms and AI...	74
6	**The System Is Failing**	79
7	**Digital Humanism and the Vienna Manifesto**	83
8	**The Digital Humanism Initiative**...............................	89
	Short History of Digital Humanism	91

9	**It's Simple, It's Complicated**	93
	Regulatory Frameworks and Legal Approaches	93
	Technical Challenges	101
10	**Conclusion**	107

Appendix: Vienna Manifesto on Digital Humanism, Vienna, May 2019 .. 109

Bibliography 113

List of Figures

Fig. 1.1	Busy subway passengers	2
Fig. 1.2	A real virtual sunset in Melbourne, St. Kilda Pier, Australia.	2
Fig. 1.3	Global GDP per capita, from the year 1 to the year 2008	4
Fig. 2.1	A neural network. (Source: Cano, A. (2017). Graphics © vielseitig.co.at)	19
Fig. 2.2	Flying straw as an obstacle for self-driving cars. (Source: Mitchell, M.: Why AI is Harder Than We Think. Digital Humanism Lecture, 22. February 2022; https://caiml.org/dighum/dighum-lectures/melaniemitchell-why-ai-is-harder-than-we-think-2022-02-22/; © Daniel Hediger)	21
Fig. 2.3	Two ways of thinking: on the right, system 1, intuitive, fast; on the left, system 2, slow, rational. (After Kahneman, 2011, Graphics © vielseitig.co.at)	22
Fig. 2.4	Three phases of "learning" of ChatGPT (Generative Pretrained Transformer): generative pretraining, finetuning, and reinforcement learning from human feedback. (© Hannes Werthner)	24
Fig. 2.5	Research and development of AI tools privatized (major AI systems by researcher affiliation). (Source: Epoch AI (2023): Parameter, Compute and Data Trends Database, CC BY 4.0, Graphics © vielseitig.co.at)	27
Fig. 2.6	Number of newly funded AI companies by geographic area, 2013–2023 (sum). (Source: Maslej et al., (2024), Graphics © vielseitig.co.at)	28
Fig. 2.7	A friendly robot. (Generative AI, Adobe Stock, file number: 801129404 © Anasaiimages, Adobe Stock)	30

Fig. 2.8	Screenshot of Weizenbaum's ELIZA—"Automatic person-centered psychotherapy". (Source: https://de.wikipedia.org/wiki/ELIZA © public domain)	31
Fig. 3.1	From the mainframe computer to the connected worldwide machine. (Source: Lecture Innovation, TU Wien, 2017 © Hannes Werthner)	42
Fig. 3.2	ENIAC, the first electronic computer in the USA. Glen Beck (Background) and Betty Snyder (Foreground) program the ENIAC. (Source: https://en.wikipedia.org/wiki/ENIAC © public domain)	44
Fig. 3.3	John von Neumann computer architecture. (Own drawing)	45
Fig. 3.4	Laws of Moore and Dennard scaling. The number of transistors on a chip has doubled every 2 years for the past 50 years. In the first half of this period, the speed also doubled with each chip generation. As the graph shows (lower line), these speed improvements ended around 2005. (Source: Evolution of Computing; https://www.researchgate.net/figure/Moores-law-and-Dennard-scaling The-number-of-transistors-on-a-chip-has-doubled-every_fig2_376715484. © Karl Rupp, CC BY 4.0)	48
Fig. 3.5	Internet usage worldwide and the digital divide (CIS Commonwealth of Independent States, an association of sovereign states, which was founded in 1991 by Russia and 11 other former Soviet republics). (Source: https://www.itu.int/itu-d/reports/statistics/2023/10/10/ff23-the-gender-digital-divide/, International Telecommunication Union (ITU). Graphics © vielseitig.co.at)	51
Fig. 3.6	Percentage of individuals owning a mobile phone, 2023. (Source: https://www.itu.int/itu-d/reports/statistics/2023/10/10/ff23-mobilephone-ownership/, International Telecommunication Union (ITU). Graphics © vielseitig.co.at)	52
Fig. 4.1	Upper image: Vilnius, separate paths for smartphone users (picturedesk.com, ID: 20180922_PD17309.	

List of Figures

	© Alexander Welscher/dpa/picturedesk.com). Lower image: Cologne, ground-mounted traffic light system—Fußgängerfurt Aachener Straße/Maarweg (Source: https://de.wikipedia.org/wiki/Bodenampel.	56
Fig. 4.2	E-commerce framework. (Source: Lecture E-Commerce, TU Wien, 2014 © Hannes Werthner)	57
Fig. 4.3	Our world of selfies and self-referentiality. "Hashtag gold medal athlete smiling for his many gadgets on selfie sticks as he poses for a picture." (Adobe Stock, File number: 92339202 © lazyllama, Adobe Stock)	59
Fig. 4.4	The increasingly dominant role of IT. (Source: Lecture Research Methods in Business Informatics, TU Wien, 2017 © Christian Huemer)	61
Fig. 5.1	From simple to complex network structures in the platform economy.	70
Fig. 5.2	The evolving AI landscape.	75
Fig. 7.1	Vitruvian Man after Leonardo da Vinci	85
Fig. 9.1	EU AI Act: AI systems are categorized according to their risk potential as unacceptable, high, limited, and minimal/no risk (Source: https://www.rtr.at/rtr/service/ki-servicestelle/ai-act/risikostufen_ki-systeme.de.html © RTR, CC BY 4.0)	96
Fig. 9.2	A link between the development of digital technologies with central questions of digital humanism, using the example of social online networks. (Source: Prem, 2024. © Erich Prem)	104
Fig. 9.3	Design and development challenges in complex systems, taking human values into consideration. (After Shneiderman, 2022. © Hannes Werthner)	105

List of Tables

Table 3.1	From numbers to a device and medium for everyone and everything	43
Table 5.1	Market capitalization (stock market value) of the top ten publicly traded companies (Financial Times Global 500)	72
Table 9.1	Digital Humanism—Research and Innovation Roadmap	102

Chapter 1
Introduction

"This is absolute nonsense" was, I remember, the reaction of the audience at the first international ENTER conference on IT and tourism, which I organized in 1994 in Innsbruck. Beat Schmid (University of St. Gallen) spoke about electronic markets, Larry Press (University of California, Los Angeles) foresaw digital agents as copies of ourselves in the digital world, and Florian Brody reflected on electronic money. The majority of the audience—both from science and industry—was very skeptical or even dismissive.[1]

Today, only 30 years later, this "nonsense" organizes and manages our life and also the world; information technology (IT) and its artifacts act as the operating system of our society, and it is hard to distinguish between the real and the virtual. We can no longer imagine a world without IT, and it contributes—apart from the fact that the world already depends on it—to solving important problems and will continue to do so in the future. However, this is also associated with serious shortcomings and undesirable developments, and in some cases, technological development is even challenging us humans—when you see how powerful artificial intelligence (AI) tools already are.

Figures 1.1 and 1.2 illustrate the rapid development very well and show our life in a physically virtual world; a clear separation is not possible anymore. Who doesn't know the situation in Fig. 1.1. The subway passengers obviously do not use their smartphones for making telephone calls only—they prefer to play games, read the news, write texts and e-mails, or listen to music. Most of these activities were previously supported by different devices (or in the case of reading books and newspapers), which were usually not available in the subway, like in the almost "ancient" times a radio or a telephone. Today, we, the passengers, have a "general"-purpose machine at hand, a computer called a smartphone.

---

[1] Today, some of the conference participants are professors (some already retired) or successful entrepreneurs.

© The Author(s), under exclusive license to Springer Nature
Switzerland AG 2025
H. Werthner, *Digital Humanism*, https://doi.org/10.1007/978-3-031-86905-1_1

Fig. 1.1 Busy subway passengers. (Urban city lifestyle and commuting in Asia, Adobe Stock, File number: 409536759 © Summit Art Creations, Adobe Stock)

Fig. 1.2 A real virtual sunset in Melbourne, St. Kilda Pier, Australia. (© Lechner 2015)

In Fig. 1.2, a scenery also well-known to us, everyone experiences the sunset through their smartphones, and what do they see? Is the sun now real or virtual? At the end, we do not care. These electronic devices become simultaneously prostheses and extensions of our (sensory) organs.

We are experiencing—and are amazed and sometimes overwhelmed by its transformative power—the complex technical, socioeconomic process known as *digital transformation*. This has happened in a short period of time, from the invention of the first electronic computer about 80 years ago to today, when our lives are no longer imaginable without IT. These systems are an essential part of public space, and everyone is (nearly) obliged to participate. This metamorphosis from a single computer to a global mega-machine affects every aspect of our lives. As Lee (2020) states, we are experiencing the co-evolution of man and machine. This disruptive development simultaneously creates and destroys, generates and destroys jobs and wealth, and improves and damages our environment. It is a dialectical socioeconomic-technical process, and in this, informatics and its "products" play a central role.

We feel at the mercy of this development, almost like a tsunami. But we should always be aware that technology and its development are neither God-given nor should they follow a technical or economic determinism. It is we, as individuals and as a society, who should determine this process. It is about us. One approach to giving us a voice and demanding equal democratic participation is digital humanism. As a concept and as an initiative with growing global support, it critically examines this development and tries to influence it.

In the following, I briefly discuss the information society and its history, and then I give an overview of the developments in the field of artificial intelligence and, somewhat more extensively, of informatics[2] as the basic science behind digital transformation. An important chapter deals with the Web, its development, and its massive impact. These "technology-induced" changes are—besides many positive effects—also associated with serious problems, which I will discuss afterward. Finally, I describe digital humanism and its Vienna Manifesto as a multidisciplinary and democratic response; it is a proactive approach that aims to integrate technical and social innovations. It can serve as a guide for future work in theory and practice.

Briefly: The Information Society

Digital transformation as a socioeconomic and technical process should be viewed in a historical context. On this large temporal scale, we see an accelerating process of change. Hanson (1998) describes how the three major "technologies" of humanity—hunting, agriculture, industry—each developed a hundred times faster than their predecessors. This growth is also very well illustrated in Fig. 1.3. It shows the growth of the growth in global gross domestic product (GDP) per capita from 1 AD to the present day.

Consider, for example, a woman who lived around AD 1 and was born again in the world around 1400 (if this were possible), when the printing press had not yet been invented. Although changed, she would essentially recognize the new world, and the changes would not really be drastic; in essence still the same technology as

---

[2] In the following, I do not distinguish, even if not entirely correct, between informatics and computer science (normally used in the Anglo-American context).

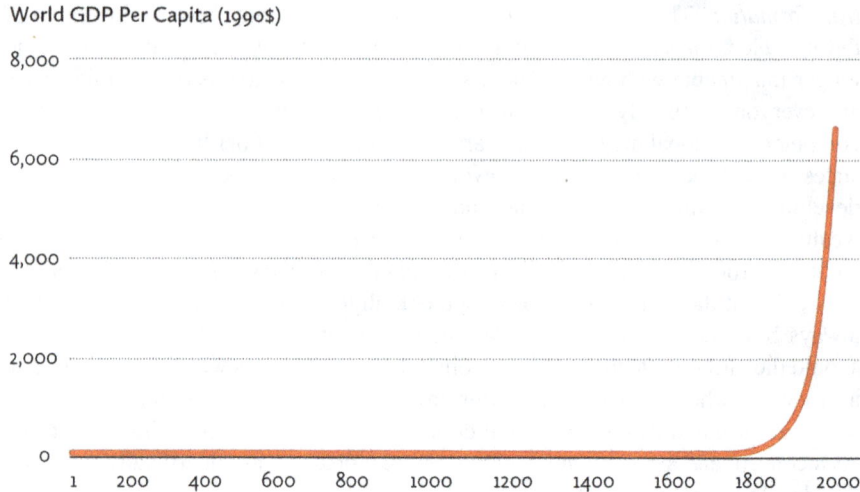

Fig. 1.3 Global GDP per capita, from the year 1 to the year 2008. (Source: Maddison Database 2010 (https://www.rug.nl/ggdc/historicaldevelopment/maddison/releases/maddison-database-2010), Graphics © vielseitig.co.at)

before, for example, no book printing press. But now think about the difference between the years 1700 and 2000. The woman would be lost because the world is completely different: cars, planes, computers, and smartphones—what is that? This growth and the acceleration described by Hanson are based on technology and innovations.

Specifically, this manifested itself from the seventeenth century onward as a series of industrial revolutions. Perez (2002) links this sequence from the steam engine and railways to steel production and electricity, then oil and the automobile, and finally to electronics and information processing, with the associated technical and economic paradigms and principles of innovation. New technologies diffuse and lead to innovation and growth (although not always for everyone). Machines increasingly take over the tasks and roles of people, energy becomes easily and flexibly available almost everywhere, and knowledge and science become an explicit factor of production. From a geographical perspective, one can observe the industrial spread up to globalization, starting in Great Britain and later in the USA. And this economic development is related to changes in political structures and institutions.[3]

Ultimately, the "information revolution" and the "computerization" of our world lead to increasing flexibility, virtualization, global real-time communication, almost unlimited mobility, network-like structures, and a further acceleration of change, as

---

[3] As shown by Acemoglu and Robinson (2012). The two authors, together with Simon Johnson, have received the Nobel Prize in Economics in 2024. Daron Acemoglu was also a guest in our Digital Humanism Lecture Series: caiml.org/dighum/dighum-lectures/daron-acemoglu-can-we-have-pro-human-ai-2024-02-13.

we experience it today. This is often referred to with the term of the *information society*, in which the creation and processing of information represent significant economic, political, and cultural activities. Authors such as Wiener (1948), Bell (1976), or Drucker (1969) use the term information society to refer to changes in society and its structure with and through new technologies and sectors; this is later often referred to as post-industrial society.

This is accompanied by a convergence of industrial sectors (see electronics and IT or the automotive industry, which today is learning, sometimes painfully, that IT is also central to them), increasing flexibility and division of labor, also on an international level (globalization with outsourcing and off-shoring enabled by the use of technical infrastructure), and the transition to the so-called service industry. Costs moved from production to marketing, and information becomes a product and knowledge a strategic resource. All of this is accompanied by an increasing differentiation of society, with a complex network of relationships and diverse interactions. As an example that may seem strange in our context, take the differentiation of cuisine into a multitude of "sub-types", but this on a global scale.

But history is not a linear, "forward" process but rather a dialectical one, full of contradictions and sometimes even reversals. This also applies to digital transformation[4] and to the information society. Here I find myself in contrast to authors like Francis Fukuyama and his famous book *End of History* (Fukuyama, 1992).

The socioeconomic-political context of this development from the 1980s onward is important. With the election of Margaret Thatcher in the United Kingdom in 1979 and Ronald Reagan in the USA in 1980, neoliberalism became the dominant political paradigm, with economic liberalization associated with privatization, deregulation, globalization, free trade, monetarism, and massive cuts in government spending. The role of the state as an institution[5] was massively downsized, and state interventions were now seen as negative. Against this background, but especially with the fall of the Berlin Wall and the decline of the Soviet Union,[6] Fukuyama made the statement that totalitarian governments had failed. Equating capitalism and democracy, he saw with the democratization of many countries in the last part of the twentieth century only capitalism and democracy as the ultimately victorious form of economic and political organization. The entire history of mankind is striving for liberal democracy as the only regime; it is *the* final form of government for all nations. Behind this argument is—besides the equation of capitalism and democracy—also a belief in the liberal market economy as *the* organizational form of goods and services exchange. A similar market optimism of the 1990s is also pursued by Thomas Friedman with his book *The World Is Flat* (Friedman, 2005),

---

[4] Rather, it should be called informatization because it informatizes almost everything.

[5] This also paved the way—probably unconsciously—for the large IT companies to take over important functions from states.

[6] It goes far beyond this book to discuss the connection between these events. However, it shows how deeply IT is intertwined with our society. To illuminate its development requires a broad view. The arms race, forced by Reagan with his *Star Wars* program, certainly also played a role in the end of the Soviet Union.

who sees the whole world as a playing field for global trade, where competitors (at least most of them) would have the same chances. Countries, companies, and individuals must remain competitive in a global market, and historical and geographical factors are less important. Consequently, he criticizes societies that resist these changes.

However, if one looks at the current situation with its many crises, such as those of the climate and the environment or the resurgence of supra-regional—hopefully not soon global—armed conflicts, as well as related fundamental differences regarding the concept of "democracy," one does not see the end of history in a positive sense. And the earth is not flat, but quite "uneven," with many holes into which one can fall deeply. Žižek (2009)—and not only he—criticizes that liberal democracy cannot be equated with capitalism, and both are not directly causally related. As a counterexample, there are some authoritarian and simultaneously capitalist successful states. Problems, triggered by the prevailing paradigm of liberal and largely unregulated market economy in large parts of the world, such as a massively unequal distribution of wealth or environmental hazards, manifested themselves in many countries in unrest against the elected governments and also in conflicts between states.

Proponents of the free market economy argue that economic efficiency[7] is achieved through the self-interest of the individual and the freedom of production and consumption, thus automatically fulfilling the interests of society as a whole. Here, one refers to the so-called first welfare theorem, which states that free markets will lead to economic efficiency under certain assumptions.[8] The assumptions made, such as perfect competition, perfect information, or no external costs, are usually not given. Thus, in practice, free markets are therefore not a guarantee for the general welfare of a society as a whole. The historical claim of the "invisible hand" by Adam Smith, according to which consumers and companies create an efficient resource allocation for the entire society by following their self-interest, obviously does not work. Therefore, the liberal democracy based on these "invisible hand" assumptions has difficulty fixing many of the problems that have arisen. The regression in many countries regarding the stability and quality of their democratic processes is related to this, as is the rise of far-right-wing political parties. Market interventions obviously seem necessary.

IT plays an important role in this development. Contrary to the great promises of the IT industry since the 1980s (this is also the time of the invention of the personal computer and the subsequent progressive digitalization), income and wealth inequality have increased in virtually all major advanced economies (Acemoglu and Restrepo, 2019; Autor, 2014; Piketty, 2021). This increase is related to the global division of labor, increasing economic and social disparities, as well as efficiency

---

[7] Put simply, economic efficiency means that goods and factors of production are distributed and allocated according to their "most valuable" uses.

[8] More specifically, it states that in economic equilibrium, complete markets with complete information and perfect competition are Pareto optimal; that is, no further exchange would make one party better off without making another worse off.

improvements and, as we will see, also to the technological development. But not only has the gap within society widened, there is also a growing gap between companies in accordance with the winner-take-all principle of the platform economy (see Chap. 5).

Furthermore, we can observe negative developments in the Web itself such as a progressive concentration with a few globally active tech giants at the center, who not only exploit (all) loopholes to avoid taxes but also exercise economic and political power. In addition, in the field of digital technologies, increased neocolonial dependencies can be observed, for example, in critical raw materials (important minerals like cobalt) or in the division of labor in the field of AI, where important steps of the training the large language models have been and are being outsourced to countries in the South—due to significantly lower labor costs there (Crawford, 2021; Tubaro et al., 2020). The global military and geopolitical conflicts must also be interpreted against the background of competition for technological supremacy and critical resources.

Technological development also affects the value of human work, which is changing due to digital transformation, as always with technological developments. The question is how this will affect us and what role people will play in the production process. With the computerization, the definition of the "input variables" in the production process is also changing: in this new world, something virtual—our personal data—seems to be becoming an important value that we humans can contribute alongside our labor force. This raises the question of whether the "surplus value" generated by humans in the work process is becoming less and less relevant and is being replaced by the added value of a never-ending stream of data, i.e., "our" behavioral traces on the Web.

In addition, contrary to the original expectations that electronic markets would lead to transparent prices, we have not achieved a transparent market where the prices "published" by all participants lead to an information-symmetric market, to optimal price discovery, with equal opportunities for all. We are drowning in a flood of data, and transparency is not given (at least for the vast majority of users). At the center of this development are the new intermediaries of the electronic world, the online platforms, and the platform economy created by them (see Chap. 5). They play a central role in the development and shaping of digital transformation—and this role was unfortunately only given the necessary attention very late.[9] It is therefore also one of the core questions of digital humanism.

As you can see, the progress of our (information) society is full of contradictions. It is a complex process that is not easy to understand and even more difficult to control. Many forces play a role, technical, societal, political, and economic. This shows that history in general, as already mentioned, is not a linear process. In

---

[9] Unfortunately, this also applies to research. To my knowledge, there is no professorship for this topic at universities in Austria, my home country. Scientific approaches to understanding the new economic rules and the mechanisms of this data-driven economy are urgently needed (apart from moral "lamenting"). Such an understanding would require a combination of several disciplines, such as computer science, statistics, sociology, economics, and political science.

addition to phases of stability and stable structures, such as the long, seemingly unchangeable on the surface, division of the world into East and West (the bipolar and cold war world), and thereafter the "end of history" (with its uni-polar "Western" world view), there are phases of social/political change and transition, where it is not clear where it is going and who is "steering" (Clark, 2023). This seems now to be case, where we are experiencing such a turbulent time, rich in political, military, and economic conflicts, moving into a multi-polar world. And this is exacerbated by the Damocles sword of the progressing environmental destruction. In this development, technology also plays a significant role. It can enable and even accelerate processes but can also contribute to conscious control. For example, AI can trigger or fuel conflicts or be used for calming. This is the larger context of digital humanism.

Chapter 2
Artificial Intelligence

Currently, we are experiencing the next wave of digitalization, artificial intelligence (AI): It highlights the contradictions of this technological development—high potential versus problematic points. However, digitalization does not end with AI; on the contrary, it is even accelerating. Almost like a tsunami, this new technology is sweeping in and over us, with truly surprising and also outstanding results. For example, GPT-4 (the product of the company OpenAI) would be at the top in university entrance tests;[1] it achieves about a result of around 88% on the American LSAT (Law School Admission Test), 89% on the SAT Math Test (for college admission), or 90% on the so-called Bar Test (entrance exam for the legal profession). And it would also successfully complete the introductory course for sommeliers with 92%, but only the theory part. Obviously, there were enough training data available. Even scientists directly involved in the research are surprised, like the Turing Prize winner[2] of 2023 and Nobel laureate of 2024, Geoffrey Hinton: "The idea that this stuff could actually get smarter than people—a few people believed that. But most people thought it was way off. And I thought it was way off. I thought it was 30 to 50 years or even longer away. Obviously, I no longer think that."[3]

---

[1] https://www.businessinsider.com/list-here-are-the-exams-chatgpt-has-passed-so-far-2023-1#gpt-4-has-a-shot-at-passing-the-cfa-exam-but-chatgpt-not-a-chance 1.

[2] The Turing Prize is the highest award in computer science. It corresponds to the Nobel Prize in other disciplines and is also only awarded once a year.

[3] https://joshuagans.substack.com/p/ai-pioneer-geoff-hinton-has-changed, retrieved on August 20, 2024.

The term artificial intelligence should actually be put in quotation marks because it attributes human qualities to a machine and thus does not differentiate between a machine and humans. This term also does not explain well how these systems work—in fact, not like humans. However, the term has become widely accepted, to the point that almost everything is now referred to as AI.

The promise of this development is obvious: a powerful tool, intelligent, flexible, and easy to use, that assists us—the people—in decision-making, technical work, and creative tasks or supplements them, such as when

- Generating and summarizing texts
- Answering questions
- Translating books[4]
- Generating photorealistic images
- Programming and creating program code
- Creating machine-based "artistic" works in image, text, audio, or video
- Creating podcasts
- Generating spoken texts with voices of predetermined speakers
- And many more …

The following concrete research results show that the use of the better information and tools provided by these new systems as input can increase the effectiveness of human skills and expertise:[5]

- Programming: Peng et al. (2023) show that software engineers can be twice as fast when using the GitHub Copilot.
- Writing tasks: According to Noy and Zhang (2023), employees with lower productivity can improve their performance in writing tasks with access to ChatGPT.
- Customer service: Brynjolfsson et al. (2023) demonstrate improvements in work productivity when ChatGPT is used in addition and provides additional information for the employees.
- Cooperation with a virtual assistant: In a study (Humlum & Vestergaard, 2024) with 100,000 employees from 11 different professions, it is estimated that ChatGPT can on average halve the time required for about a third of the work tasks.

These specific application examples show the character of AI as GPT (General Purpose Technology).[6] This is not surprising, as it is a product of informatics, which is also "general." AI can and will be used for all purposes—as we describe above—and shaped according to the respective task. Therefore, it "permeates" all areas of our lives. This also explains—among other factors—the great hopes placed in AI and the high economic potential. For example, McKinsey predicts that this technology could generate an additional economic output of around 13 trillion US dollars by 2030 and increase global GDP by about 1.2% annually.[7]

---

[4] As in the case of this book.
[5] See Acemoglu, D.: Can we have pro-human AI? Digital Humanism lecture, February 13, 2024; https://dighum.org/dighum-lectures/daron-acemoglu-can-we-have-pro-human-ai-2024-02-13/.
[6] Technology that can be used for "everything" or for general purposes.
[7] https://www.mckinsey.com/featured-insights/artificial-intelligence/notes-from-the-ai-frontier--modeling-the-impact-of-ai-on-the-world-economy—but what hasn't been predicted already.

But: There Is No Free Lunch

With the launch of OpenAI's ChatGPT in November 2022, we became unsolicited participants in a worldwide, unannounced experiment. By January 2023, there were 100 million users; currently, the chatbot records about 1.5 billion visits per month.[8] As a researcher, one may think of the quite huge effort that one has to put into one's own research in experiments with humans or surveys, from consent forms to ethics boards. In the computer industry, when launching software products, this is apparently not the case.

The chatbot ChatGPT, based on the LLM GPT (Large Language Model named Generative Pretrained Transformer[9]), also clearly shows the problems of this new AI, based on a massive amount data and on machine learning with deep neural networks:

- **Hallucination**: These systems "hallucinate." However, this is not entirely correct. Hallucinating presupposes that one knows what is true and what is not true. This is not the case here; this systems have no notion of truth. And this is not a bug; it is a feature of these systems. It invents, creates believable and consistent fiction, and even invents quotes. **It is a story and not a truth machine**. But its stories are consistent, which makes it hard to notice anything. The statements are, without explicitly mentioning it, "probability" statements. Therefore, ChatGPT necessarily also generates false information. If the computer was understood up to now as the embodiment of the "secure" statement or problem solution, it now turns around—the human must check the truth content. And the system can also be used explicitly abusively:

    – Disinformation—deliberate or also unconscious—can contribute to the destabilization of societies. This applies in general, but with AI, this can now be almost automated and significantly facilitated. Especially consciously produced fake news can manipulate and polarize societies as well. An example among many are "pictures" of Taylor Swift as a supporter of Donald Trump during his electoral campaign in the USA in 2024. There is already a separate industry for this type of communication, the disinformation industry. However, the story of misinformation is a long one, starting long before the Internet—see, for example, (Cortada & Aspray, 2019) who offer a powerful historical corrective to those who claim we are now in a new "post-truth" era. And there are also voices warning against overemphasizing these effects or noting that fears that generative AI-driven disinformation is gaining the upper hand have not yet come true. However, AI-generated content has often massively been used for spam and pornography.[10]

---

[8] https://doit.software/de/blog/chatgpt-statistiken#screen3.

[9] GPT stands for two different things: Generative Pretrained Transformer (a specific AI product) and General Purpose Technology.

[10] Ninety-eight percent of all deepfake videos on the Internet are of a pornographic nature.

- The European police agency Europol warns in a report published in The Hague of the criminal misuse of text robots based on LLMs. The technology could be used for fraud, misinformation, and cybercrime.[11]
- The company Discord used OpenAI technology for their own AI-driven chatbot. Users were then able to use it through clever questioning to output or generate information that should actually be protected. Some managed to get the system to output instructions for the production of the illegal drug methamphetamine and the incendiary device napalm. Or researchers at Anthropic found it surprisingly easy to bypass the safety measures of language models like ChatGPT. Using a simple algorithm called Best-of-N Jailbreaking, they succeeded to trick the models into generating harmful content, e.g., how to build a bomb.[12]
- A lawyer in the USA used ChatGPT for a court application and unknowingly relied on invented judgments. A court application contained references to "specific" cases, including alleged judgments and file numbers, which were made up.[13]

- **The result or the path to the solution is not comprehensible—the system acts as a black box.** There is currently no way to determine and to understand how the system arrived at its decision. This poses one of the biggest research questions of this generative AI.

  - The internal workings and decision-making processes of the AI system are opaque and not understandable to humans. In other words, when you input data into the AI system and receive results, you don't really know how the AI arrived at the conclusions it presents. And more importantly, you don't know if the result is correct. Take an autonomous vehicle as an example: if it hits a pedestrian, even though you would expect it to brake in time, we cannot understand the process of the system due to its black box nature and see why it made this decision. This lack of transparency is one of the biggest concerns associated with type of data-driven AI. This is also why alarm bells are ringing at regulatory authorities. There are legitimate concerns about whether we can trust AI systems. The lack of transparency also raises many questions about accuracy. Lack of transparency makes it practically very difficult to test and validate the results of black box AI models.

- **Bias** occurs in several forms, which, however, mix with each other. When using it, one has no knowledge about the data selection, i.e., which data were used how. Even if one knows from which areas the data come, one is in the dark whether a

---

[11] https://www.zeit.de/digital/internet/2023-03/chatgpt-europol-missbrauch-kriminelle-kuenstliche-intelligenz.

[12] techcrunch.com/2023/04/20/jailbreak-tricks-discords-new-chatbot-into-sharing-napalm-and-meth-instructions.

[13] https://www.zdf.de/nachrichten/panorama/chatgpt-anwalt-klage-gericht-antrag-recherche-scheitern-100.html.

"correct" selection of the data used for training the models was made, i.e., a "correct sampling" in relation to the entirety to be modeled. The training data usually come from the "net," where they are freely available or are considered as such. However, the Web itself is characterized by the so-called Wisdom of the few (Baeza-Yates & Murgai, 2024), where most people only observe and few actively contribute to the content (see Nielsen's 90-9-1 *Participation Rule*, where 1% of users create content; 9% engage with it, such as through comments or likes; and 90% just watch). So few determine the content. Another example of distorted data: In 2009, 7% of Facebook users produced 50% of the content; in 2013, it was only 4% at Amazon who created 50% of the reviews. And ultimately there is a "general" distortion of the data by the demographics of the users: estimates suggest that 60% of the ten million best Web sites are in English, but only 5% of the world's population have English as their mother tongue (13% speak English). These data distortions then lead to misclassifications and also—in the case of generative methods—to poor reproductions. An example is the AI-generated images of former US presidential candidate Kamala Harris, which are easily recognizable as fakes. The reason is that certain, non-white population groups are underrepresented in the data. A future and then serious problem arises from the fact that, according to estimates[14] in 2026, 90% of all online content will be generated by AI. This means a loss of diversity with probably large but currently difficult estimable impacts on the quality of the trained language models. It also points at the issue that AI companies run data—they always need more and more data (see later). Another problem related to the data is the almost "free" use of data by AI companies, with many cases of plagiarism—something that is currently being dealt with in court.[15]

AI: A Discussion Between Dystopia and Utopia

It is interesting to note that the Global North is currently rather pessimistic about AI, while the countries of the Global South, including Asia, are much more optimistic.[16] And overall, according to the Edelman Trust Barometer (2024)[17], trust in AI companies worldwide has fallen from 61% (5 years ago) to 53%, especially in the USA from 50% to 35%, during the period of great success. It is interesting that the mood

---

[14] www.europol.europa.eu/cms/sites/default/files/documents/Europol_Innovation_Lab_Facing_Reality_Law_Enforcement_And_The_Challenge_Of_Deepfakes.pdf?

[15] 59.7% of GPT-3.5 results contained some form of plagiarized content; copyleaks.com/about-us/media/copyleaks-research-finds-nearly-60-of-gpt-3-5-outputs-contained-some-form-of-plagiarized-content.

[16] https://www.axios.com/2024/03/12/western-countries-ai-generative-ai-productivity. According to the conducting company YouGov, 67% of people in India believe that AI has improved overall productivity at their workplace, in Indonesia 65%, and in the UAE 62%. At the bottom of the list are Sweden (14%), the USA (17%), and the UK (18%).

[17] https://www.edelman.com/trust/2024/trustbarometer

is more negative in the countries of "AI research and development"[18] and that trust seems to have fallen with the success of the research. In terms of content, the following positions can be roughly identified in the international discussion on the evaluation of AI:

- **Business as usual**: In the history of computer science, there have been many hypes, such as expert systems or decision support systems. Here, exaggerated hopes were often raised, which then did not materialize to the hoped or expected extent. The position of business as usual also refers to a flattening of user growth (at a high level) as well as the performance flattening of the large language models (LLMs).[19] The massive stock market decline of August 5, 2024, is also argued with the overheated expectations in the AI sector. In addition, there are voices that at least question the AI revolution.[20] However, in general, the stock markets experienced a boom in 2024. In the USA, Japan, Germany, Great Britain, and France, the leading indices reached new record highs during the year, with the major technology companies as the biggest winners.
- **Warnings of existential threats**: This position assumes a high probability of the emergence of **AGI** (artificial general intelligence; see later). This would mean expecting machines that are superior to "humans" and could therefore also exterminate them. This fear was also echoed in the open letter from the Future of Life Institute, which called for a moratorium in the field of AI—which, however, no one complied with.[21]
- In contrast, there are the **Hype Warners** like Meredith Whittaker from Signal or Timnit Gebru (formerly Google), who identify these previous fears as "warning hype." As they say, they may also serve to distract from the real problems, such as dangers like surveillance, misinformation, or economic concentration.
- And finally, there are **the cautious ones** who see great potential but warn of the negative social and economic consequences and want to "control" them. Ultimately, their question is: who decides on research and application? This corresponds to the digital humanism position.

Singularity and Strong vs. Weak AI

This question of the assessment of AI is behind the previously mentioned different positions in the current AI discussion. This means:

---

[18] Both are concentrated in a few countries; more on this later.

[19] https://www.reddit.com/r/mlscaling/comments/1ebrkin/closedsource_vs_openweight_models/?rdt=45319.

[20] The *Economist*: What happened to the artificial-intelligence revolution? July 2, 2024.

[21] https://futureoflife.org/open-letter/pause-giant-ai-experiments/.

- **Weak AI**: Here, AI is limited to solving well-defined, predetermined problems and does not claim general intelligence.
- **AGI (artificial general intelligence)** or **strong AI**: A program can understand or learn to solve **any** intellectual task that a human can perform, and this also includes the possibility of sentience and consciousness. If one follows this view or assesses the capabilities of AI in this way, then AI systems can build new systems, better and better, until they ultimately exceed human capabilities. This would then bring us to the point called "singularity," a bifurcation point in the history of human development (Kurzweil, 2005). However, Geoffrey Hinton pointed to the current acceleration in AI research and estimated the probability that AI will lead to the extinction of humanity within the next three decades at 10–20% (some time ago, he estimated it at "only" 10%).[22]

But you can also take a pragmatic position, which is probably shared by most scientists, such as the leading researchers Stuart Russell and Peter Norvig: They are interested in how a program behaves in concrete terms and what it can do in concrete terms; and if it behaves as if it had intelligence, then you need to know whether it really does.

Brief excursion to posthumanism[23] with such representatives as Ray Kurzweil: This is about overcoming the current stage of human development. Representatives of posthumanism argue that an AI will replace humans after the singularity. It is about a future beyond the biological body and a new human after the human. Thus, with the singularity, something like the separation of mind and body occurs, with the immortality of the mind. Here, there are also scenarios of "brain uploading." Interestingly, this direction resembles the Christian religion, which also separates soul and body and assumes the immortality of the former. However, the question remains: what role then does the "original" human take on, if it still exists? Will it be extinguished—or if not, can everyone afford this technical immortality, or does it remain limited to a caste of the haves? In the past, before the period of enlightenment and science, we humans used religion to get an explanation for the unexplainable. Will this role of religion be taken over by AI after the singularity (if we humans still exist)?

What Is AI?

In the 2023 EU AI Act, an "AI system" is defined as follows:

> [...] a machine-based system that is designed to operate with varying levels of autonomy and that may exhibit adaptiveness after deployment, and that, for explicit or implicit objectives, infers, from the input it receives, how to generate outputs such as predictions, content, recommendations, or decisions that can influence physical or virtual environments.[24]

---

[22] BBC Radio 4, December 27, 2024.

[23] Or more precisely, of technological posthumanism—a thorough discussion of these currents, also in distinction to transhumanism, is not the subject of this book.

[24] https://artificialintelligenceact.eu/article/3/.

This definition is unfortunately almost incomprehensible and actually includes any more or less complex software and hardware system—the difficulty is that it is almost impossible to narrow it down. Doesn't any software run to a certain degree autonomously, controlled by input data, and doesn't it have effects on the environment, by regulating, e.g., a power plant? But the law requires a definition of what it regulates.

Probably Haigh's (2024) view is more accurate, who describes AI as a common "brand" or ensemble of related IT-based technologies that perform complex tasks, with some similarity to human behavior. This comprehensive view is also fueled by the market and sales interests of the IT industry. Today, almost everything is referred to as AI; this attracts attention and increases sales chances. This, however, can also be observed in the academic community, where specific fields of research such as recommender systems are now treated as a field of AI, what nobody would have done a few years ago.

I see AI as the simulation of human behavior; the machine shows intelligent characteristics to us as observers. In other words, it is the "automation" of thinking, "materialized" in code (software and hardware).[25] Ultimately, this leads to the question of human intelligence, which I will not answer here. But intelligence does not only affect mental processes but also physical and emotional ones, and it is also socially and culturally as well as physically "embedded."

The discussion becomes clearer when I subsequently come to the different methods of AI and then define AI as systems that use these methods.[26] The term artificial intelligence also includes a human attribution to computer systems. It does not separate between human and machine; it is an anthropomorphic term and attributes human characteristics to the machine.[27]

The birth of AI is considered to be the Dartmouth Conference in New Hampshire, USA, in 1956, with today's world-famous participants such as Marvin Minsky, John McCarthy, Claude Shannon, Allen Newell, or Herbert Simon.[28] There, the term artificial intelligence was established. In the funding application for the conference, a two-month seminar was proposed, which assumes that "every aspect of learning or any other feature of intelligence can in principle be so precisely described that a machine can be made to simulate it. An attempt will be made to find how to make machines use language, form abstractions and concepts, solve kinds of problems now reserved for humans, and improve themselves."[29] This is, in my view, a better definition of AI than the one found in the EU AI Act.[30]

---

[25] Due to these ambiguities, there are many definitions, such as "AI refers to computer systems capable of performing complex tasks that in the past could only be done by humans, e.g., logical thinking, decision-making, or problem-solving."

[26] Whether this helps remains to be seen.

[27] See also the criticism of using the term "intelligence" by Jaron Lanier, one of the pioneers of computer science (https://www.newyorker.com/science/annals-of-artificial-intelligence/how-to-picture-ai).

[28] As far as it is known, there were no female participants.

[29] http://www-formal.stanford.edu/jmc/history/dartmouth/dartmouth.html; see also https://de.wikipedia.org/wiki/Dartmouth_Conference.

[30] There was also a "competing concept" or notion to AI, namely, cybernetics, defined by MIT scientist Norbert Wiener. It means the "science of communication and control." However, Wiener thought of cybernetics in terms of analog systems and not the digital computers, something that the

The whole thing was associated with many expectations; see, for example, Marvin Minsky, 1967—"Within a generation, I am convinced [...] the problem of creating 'artificial intelligence' will be substantially solved"—or Herbert Simon, 1965: "machines will be capable, within twenty years, of doing any work a man can do." However, over time, a certain disillusionment set in, for example with John McCarthy, in 2006: "Human-level AI is harder than it seemed." In these years, since 1956, there have been several so-called AI summers and winters, depending on how successful one was in research and, above all, in application. This only changed again in recent years with the breakthrough in machine learning and deep neural networks.

The Two Methods of AI

Essentially, there are two major method classes of AI, and all definitions of AI implicitly assume their use.

Symbolic or Logic-Based AI

It is based on mathematical logic and describes the world as a set of a priori given facts and rules. These facts and rules constitute the so-called knowledge base. From this knowledge base, conclusions are then drawn through a logical procedure using inference rules in a causal process—a mechanism that was already described and developed by the Greeks, beginning with Aristotle. This method was the core of AI for decades, with the extension of probabilistic rules, multi-valued logic, or the ability to resolve contradictory statements.

A trivial example:
IF **Fever** is **yes**
AND **Cough** is **yes**
AND **Runny Nose** is **yes**
AND **Headache** is **yes**

THEN **Diagnosis** is **Flu**.[31]

---

others who drafted the proposal advocated. Moreover, the organizers had a problem with Wiener's personality as a superstar at the time. History is thus also a story of individuals and coincidences. https://punyamishra.com/2024/07/10/cybernetics-or-ai-whats-in-a-name/.

[31] If all characteristics apply (i.e., are true), then one has the flu (and certainly so). However, this would probably also apply to COVID-19, so the rule would need to be updated. As you can see, rule-based systems are not as simple as presented here.

The advantage of this method is obvious. You can understand these conclusions, and the results are clear and guaranteed. You see, informatics loves clarity; it helps in the search for truth. Also, the knowledge base is explicitly accessible and verifiable. The method works almost like a virtual mechanistic machine: Once properly built, the true statements are automatically derived from the ingredients.

However, important questions arise: Is everything in this world a priori and explicitly describable by a set of formal rules and facts? Can these also be recognized and formulated? This is called the problem of knowledge acquisition. Then, once the problem is formulated, do the derived solutions still have anything to do with the (real) world?[32]

A further problem is that over time, this set of rules and facts explodes[33]—the system does not scale and has its limits with really big problems like automatic language translation or pattern recognition. However, rule-based systems show very good results in areas like scheduling or automatic diagnosis of technical systems—these are fields where problems can be formally described.

Sub-symbolic AI

This approach starts with the data in "some" form,[34] and from there, "learning" is then done using statistical methods, i.e., patterns and relationships between data are recognized. Thus, sub-symbolic AI refers to methods that process information using distributed, low-level representations instead of explicit symbols or logical reasoning. In this "data-driven" or "data-based" AI, neural networks are mainly used, which were proposed as early as 1943 by McCulloch and Pitts, who modeled the neuronal structures of our brains (McCulloch & Pitts, 1943).

This approach can basically be seen as the reverse process: we have an enormous amount of data, and we learn something about the world from this. Although there have been and are major successes in pattern recognition and medicine, this approach was for years, in the shadow of logicians, the other method. The main problem is that one cannot really understand how the system arrives at its solution—that it works as a **black box**. You see the input-output behavior, but you do not know how it works internally.

---

[32] Moreover, predicate logic, one of the most important methods of this type of AI, is generally undecidable: There are formal logical statements that can neither be proven nor refuted. So not all formally describable problems have a formal solution.

[33] To my knowledge, the largest system, Cyc by Doug Lenat, has a knowledge base of about 24 million rules and assumptions and was mostly manually created over 1000 person-years (en.wikipedia.org/wiki/Cyc).

[34] Of course, this is not really correct. The data must, after being selected by humans, of course be processed and converted into a "machine-readable" form.

The system works as follows (see Fig. 2.1): The input (e.g., image of a cat) is converted into signals (numbers). The picture consists of pixels. It is a rectangle consisting of individual cells, the pixels. Each pixel is becoming an input signal. These signals move from level to level of the network from left to right until the output is the classification of the object in the image, e.g., cat yes/no (Fig. 2.1, upper part). There is the input layer, one or more hidden layers, and the output layer. If a neural network has a particularly large number of hidden layers, then we have arrived at "deep learning." The network consists of nodes (neurons) that receive information from other neurons via the synapses (connections) or from outside. The information on the edges is weighted (the weights w in Fig. 2.1), then processed in the neuron using the transition function (e.g., a summation), and then passed on as "its" result (lower part of Fig. 2.1). Of course, not all results are correct at the beginning. However, these errors are calculable—as is the contribution of an

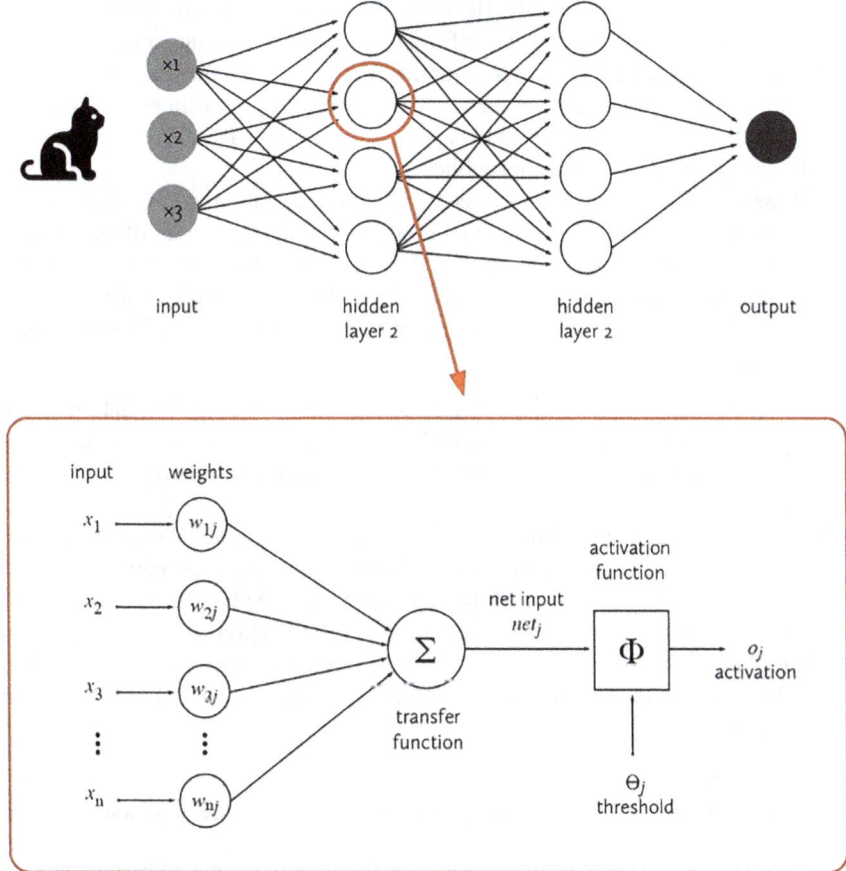

Fig. 2.1 A neural network. (Source: Cano, A. (2017). Graphics © vielseitig.co.at)

individual neuron to the error—and are then minimized in the next training cycle by changing the weights of the respective neurons and synapses accordingly. In this way, the network learns with each training cycle. In so-called supervised learning, the training data consists of input data and the known and correct output. The network is run through, and parameters are corrected until the correct specified result is achieved. Unsupervised learning, the second major type of machine learning, trains the model on unlabeled data, and there are no predefined categories or outputs. The system tries to infer patterns, structure, or features from the data without guidance, similar to cluster analysis in statistics. As you can see, it all depends on this data and its selection.[35]

Machine learning systems recognize patterns in the data, not explicit rules how the data are related. So after pattern recognition, they do not "know" that a cat has two ears, four legs, fur, a tail, and interesting-looking eyes—that is, that an object without these features is not a cat. For humans, however, the steps to the result are not comprehensible without such rules. In a certain sense, neural networks program themselves with the training data. However, the underlying learning program—i.e., how the machine recognizes patterns from data—comes from humans. In a certain way, we use the past to predict the future. But the way we represent data or which we select is the way we perceive the world—they reflect our assumptions including our prejudices. From this perspective, these systems also have an "enlightening" quality; they make our prejudices public.

These systems show great success in medicine, in pattern recognition, in language processing, and translation. For example, the detection rate of skin cancer diseases could be significantly increased by machine learning methods. In the corona pandemic, these methods also helped speed up the research of new vaccines, and they also supported the personalization of medical treatment. This success is based on:

- Big data: Enormous increase in available data, of the Web and its data with the possibility of accessing it. So, the Web and the big search engines, which make the huge amount of data available and accessible, are the precondition of this "new" AI.
- Increased hardware performance, both in terms of storage and computing power, including parallelization and cheap GPUs (graphics processing units).
- Software: Improved methods of machine learning in the last 20 years, for example, by the Turing Prize winners of 2018, Geoffrey Hinton, Yoshua Bengio, and Yann LeCun, for their work in the field of deep learning (in the 1990s), or then in 2017 by the Google researchers (Vaswani et al., 2017) with their work on attention.[36]

---

[35] For more information on deep learning and neural networks, see Aggarwal (2023) or Schmidhuber (2015).

[36] The attention mechanism in machine learning helps figure out which parts of the input are most important for a task so they can focus on those. It works by giving more weight to the important parts and less to the rest. This makes the system smarter at understanding context, which matters most.

Since the beginning of AI, the logic-based approach has been predominant, also because of its proximity to theoretical computer science and the "necessity" to deliver secure and explainable results. Geoffrey Hinton referred to this situation in an interview with the *MIT Technology Review* (May 2, 2023): "Back in the 1980s, neural networks were a joke." This has now radically changed, and the sub-symbolic approach is now often mistakenly equated with AI.

Everything Possible?

The systems recognize patterns in data, but they fundamentally have difficulty abstracting general knowledge from the data; for example, in the form of rules or relationships between concepts described in terms of content, such terms as "mother" and "son" are more closely related than "son" and "jaguar." In addition, everyday knowledge or something like "common sense reasoning" is lacking.

A self-driving car has difficulties recognizing that it could drive through this flying straw (Fig. 2.2). In contrast, humans can use this knowledge from their everyday knowledge. Or as Cho (2023) stated: "Common sense is the dark matter of AI." Furthermore, it can happen that a small change to an image that is not recognizable to us humans (e.g., a pixel changes the value) causes the neural network to

Fig. 2.2 Flying straw as an obstacle for self-driving cars. (Source: Mitchell, M.: Why AI is Harder Than We Think. Digital Humanism Lecture, 22. February 2022; https://caiml.org/dighum/dighum-lectures/melaniemitchell-why-ai-is-harder-than-we-think-2022-02-22/; ©Daniel Hediger)

misclassify. This can then also be used for attacks on a system (so-called adversarial attacks).

Two Methods: Two Ways of Thinking[37]

Figure 2.3 shows that the two methods of AI resemble the two human ways of thinking: slow and conscious versus fast and automatic. System 1 according to Kahneman (2011) is intuitive, fast, rather unconscious and makes quick, sometimes inexplicable decisions. System 2, on the other hand, corresponds to the slow and rational decision-making process. These two opposing ways of thinking also complement each other, which is essential for our thinking and decision-making processes. We humans are often forced to make unconscious decisions—think of our unconscious actions while driving, where we cannot always wait for seconds for the results of rational process. Neural networks correspond to system 1—fast and simultaneously "black box"—the logic-based and conscious, comprehensible approach corresponds to system 2. However, unlike "humans," we as researchers have not yet succeeded in building systems that integrate both types of AI processes. But in both methods, the human plays the decisive role: In logical systems, we define how we formally see the world and which rules we take; in the data-driven approach, we also decide, namely, with the selection of the data we use to train the systems.

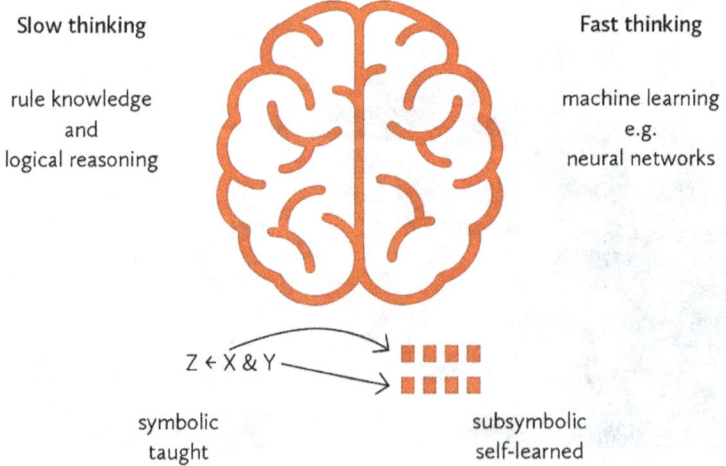

Fig. 2.3 Two ways of thinking: on the right, system 1, intuitive, fast; on the left, system 2, slow, rational. (After Kahneman, 2011, Graphics © vielseitig.co.at)

---

[37] Thanks to my colleague Edward A. Lee for pointing out this comparison.

And Now LLM (Large Language Model)

LLMs as the next step in AI are essentially improved methods of machine and deep learning. These models[38] form the basis of the current hype in AI. They are based on so-called deep learning networks—neural networks with up to over 100 intermediate levels,[39] and they are extended by new methods such as the transformer architecture[40] and the "self-attention" mechanism. An LLM provides—given an input (word, paragraph, image, etc.)—as output the prediction of the most likely next word, sentence, paragraph, or even part of an image. But in correct terms, it is not about words but actually about so-called tokens. Simplified tokens are the "basic units" of the LLM, into which every piece of information, i.e., word or image as well as computer code (which is also used for learning programming), is broken down or converted into. LLMs are essentially trained for a single task: predicting the next token, i.e., predict the probability of the nth token, given the previous n − 1 tokens as input. In the case of text, when a text fragment is entered, they output which word might continue and with what probability. In a certain respect, this resembles a complex autocomplete, as we know it from search engines.

The LLM or the core of it is a "mapping" of language onto a huge network of statistical relationships between all tokens of the provided input data. Since these data contain many different languages and also images, an LLM maps these languages—and in the multimodal case images—simultaneously in a huge network; it is multilingual by design. The computation of these relationships is extremely complex. This is also the reason why LLMs are so large and why so many training data are needed. The statistical relationships, done by a so-called word embedding,[41] naturally also reflect the semantic-content ones ("queen" is "closer" to "king" than "tractor"). However, these are not explicitly recognizable, at least for us humans. An analogy would be a huge forest, or rather a jungle, where well-trodden paths correspond to frequently used sentences and less used sentences correspond to less well-trodden paths. Based on these probabilities for all possible tokens, it is then calculated which continuations of inputs (sequence of written texts including structure, style) are output. So, an LLM receives the first part of a sentence as input, i.e., "prompt," and outputs the hypothetical continuation.

---

[38] A model is understood to be a representation of a system. It serves to understand the behavior of the real system and to explain it. Therefore, the term "model" in LLMs is not really correct. An LLM does not "understand" and explain human language.

[39] These numbers are not disclosed by the resp. companies.

[40] The transformer architecture is a newly developed, very efficient deep learning architecture of machine learning, developed by Google, which integrates a so-called attention mechanism. The latter ensures that certain parts of the input receive special attention during processing—it pays attention to the specific context of the elements to be processed (Vaswani et al., 2017).

[41] Word embedding is a method of representing words as unique codes (in mathematical terms vectors) that capture their meanings and relationships. It helps computers recognize similarities between words.

Through training with a large corpus of documents, consisting of text, code, images, and audio, the system learns to provide appropriate responses. If an output is wrong in the learning process, a learning algorithm—in this case, one called self-supervised learning—updates the network parameters until a target criterion is met. In self-supervised learning, the system learns by predicting parts of the data from other parts, creating its own labels from the input data. It thus bridges the gap between supervised and unsupervised learning by generating labels automatically, without requiring human annotation. It reduces the need for large amounts of labeled data but requires instead larger datasets and longer training times.

An LLM "learns" language without knowing the grammar or its rules at all, i.e., how to form sentences, what an adjective or a verb is, etc. It is a statistical representation of our language based on the data available for training.[42] The output generated by the generative AI can therefore be seen as a variation or recombination of existing content.

Figure 2.4 shows the sequence of learning of ChatGPT, starting with the process of learning how the system can generate text itself; then it is fine-tuned to a specific task, and finally, it receives feedback from people to get even better. The first step is generative pretraining: here, the system recognizes words (i.e., tokens) and connections between words based on a huge amount of text (from books, Web sites, etc.). Basic patterns and relationships in the language are recognized. The result is the so-called foundational model, which can then be adapted to a variety of tasks. This next step is fine-tuning by supervised learning with well-curated datasets. In this phase, the model is trained on specific tasks, such as a conversational chat. The idea is to better tailor it to the user's expectations and reduce it to the defined task. The examples of the dataset should ensure coherent, safe, and contextually relevant responses, as well as avoid harmful content.

In the third step, the system uses so-called reinforcement learning from human feedback (RLHF), in which human trainers evaluate the answers suggested by the system and thereby improve them. The human feedback is used to train a reward model that scores the outputs based on desirability. In such a way, the training by humans also serves to prevent "unpleasant" or offensive responses. These final

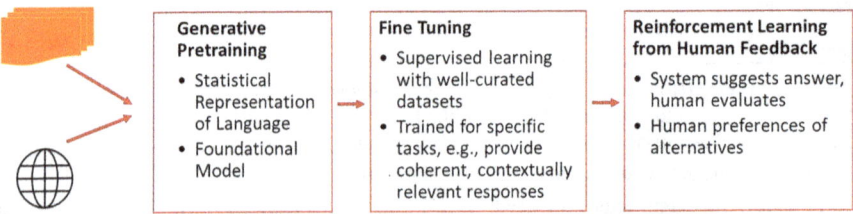

Fig. 2.4 Three phases of "learning" of ChatGPT (Generative Pretrained Transformer): generative pretraining, finetuning, and reinforcement learning from human feedback. (© Hannes Werthner)

---

[42] One can also say that a LLM does know the language.

steps, where humans are necessary, were mostly and are outsourced to countries in the Global South due to low labor costs.

These generative models represent an essential further development of machine learning; while machine learning was originally used for analysis and classification, it is now also used to generate "new" content. Technically formulated, a discriminative model (original machine learning) can be used to estimate the probability of whether the object in the image is a cat or—an example from tourism—whether I like a vacation spot or not. The new generative models, on the other hand, can create a description of a destination that I might like.[43]

An important distinction between a logic-based and a machine learning approach in AI arises from system theory and the underlying model "strengths." The logic-based AI corresponds to a so-called structural model: It has the same input-output behavior as the natural system, and it possesses additionally a structural interior, derived from the observation of the real system. Thus, the model can also explain the natural system and how it works. In contrast, the machine learning approach corresponds to a so-called functional system: it shows the same input-output behavior as the natural system, but has no insight into the internal processes or structure of the system. It can therefore not explain how results are obtained. Ironically, neural networks were introduced because they resemble the structure of the human brain and were supposed to help explain its functioning. They are today the far more effective methods of AI.

What Is Knowledge?

GPT-3 from OpenAI has 175 billion parameters[44] (for GPT-4, numbers are not provided), as a result of training with an enormous amount of data. In a certain sense, this is the "knowledge"—and not the software. One could also imagine this as a huge EXCEL-CSV file. This knowledge is implicit, human reading of this data is not possible, and it makes no "sense"; it does not represent a human-understandable model. But the performance is amazing. For example, the AI from DeepMind (Google) predicts the weather faster and more accurately without explicit knowledge and model than the classic approaches that model the physical processes in the atmosphere.[45]

In contrast to well-structured databases or classical knowledge bases, which represent data exactly, where data can be indexed and retrieved, LLMs act as a kind of completion machine and complete the entered data in a probabilistic way—as an approximate answer. They have no model of the physical world and no everyday

---

[43] Thanks to Francesco Ricci for this hint.

[44] Parameter correspond more or less to the weights on the synapses (the connection between two neurons). But neural networks have also additional parameters, which do not have a direct biological equivalent.

[45] https://www.nature.com/articles/d41586-023-03552-y.

knowledge, nor can they plan hierarchically. They can only respond precisely to input prompts if they have been fed with the right training data; they are "inherently uncertain."

On the other hand, in many areas—as described—they achieve excellent, unexpected results and are finding their way into all areas in which software is now used. It is interesting to note that the fact that this type of problem-solving surpasses classical model-based approaches has not yet led—astonishingly—to a massive discussion in the theory of science. Science is also the creation of models about the object of study (be it physical or abstract) in order to make statements about it, to understand it, and possibly also to predict its future. This is not the case in this new form of AI. It works and solves a problem, but what is our finding? LLMs are therefore not only a challenge for science but also for computer science, which assumes deterministic machines, with clear, guaranteed solutions. This proves to be not applicable here. This AI may also be the representative of a new "computational paradigm."

Although I reject the mechanistic worldview (see Chap. 7), it is interesting to do a purely "physical" comparison with the human brain. Our brain has a huge number of synapses; estimates go up to 10^{11} (one hundred billion) neurons. Each of these can have thousands—on average 7000—synaptic connections (synapses) to other neurons. Estimates for an adult vary and range from 10^{14} to 5×10^{14} synapses (100–500 trillion). However, a direct comparison with LLMs—here we take GPT—is difficult, partly because many figures have not been published. Here, the estimate for GPT4 for the number of connections (synapses)—comparable to the weights between the artificial neurons—is a few trillion. This is much smaller and therefore less flexible than the human brain, which in addition is constantly forming and adapting new connections.

In terms of power consumption, our brain is ultra-efficient, requiring about 20 W (continuous power) for all thought processes, creativity, and sensory processing. GPT-4 is estimated to require up to 1 kWh of energy per prompt (input), depending on model size and computational complexity. This shows that the brain remains undisputedly more efficient in terms of energy consumption and calculations per watt.

What Is the Effort: Who Can Afford This?

Here are some numbers, which however change continuously due to the technological dynamics:[46]

GPT-4 from OpenAI

- Trained with trillions of words
- More than one trillion parameters and a network with 120 layers (estimated)

---

[46] Regarding costs for end users or companies: there are different cost models, from free use to subscription models.

- Ten million queries per day
- Estimated duration of model training: 34 days

Gemini from Google has also over one trillion parameters (in case of the model Gemini Ultra). All of this is of course associated with high costs. The effort for OpenAI to run its GPT models (including ChatGPT) is about $700,000 per day. This includes computing resources, infrastructure, maintenance, and continuous improvements to the models. The cost of training GPT-4 is estimated at about $63–$78.4 million (Google's Gemini Ultra cost is $191 million for compute). This includes expenditures for the extensive datasets, consisting of about 13 trillion tokens, used for training, as well as for the hardware needed to manage and process large amounts of data.[47]

These enormous costs (plus personnel and knowledge costs) lead to a highly concentrated AI landscape, where a few well-known companies dominate, such as Microsoft/OpenAI, Google (Alphabet), Apple, Samsung, Nvidia, Amazon, Meta (Facebook), Alibaba, or Tencent. But there is also a vivid start-up ecosystem, where, however, many of those are related with one of the big players (see Fig. 2.6). The dominance of private companies is also illustrated by the following figures: In 2023, industry produced 51 notable machine learning models, while academia contributed only 15 (Maslej et al., 2024), and 50% of the datasets used come from only 12 institutions (10 of which are in the USA). The public sector plays a subordinate role in this development: In 2021, the ratio of expenditures in this area between public and private (limited to the USA and the EU) was 1:100 (Ahmed et al., 2023). Figure 2.5 shows the growing dominance of the industry (either alone or, to a lower extent, in cooperation with universities—both together over 80%) and the relative decline of

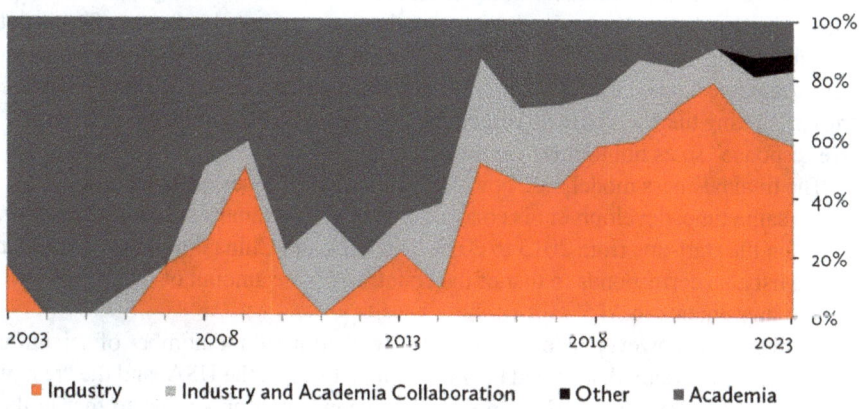

Fig. 2.5 Research and development of AI tools privatized (major AI systems by researcher affiliation). (Source: Epoch AI (2023): Parameter, Compute and Data Trends Database, CC BY 4.0, Graphics © vielseitig.co.at)

---

[47] Response from ChatGPT from August 2, 2024.

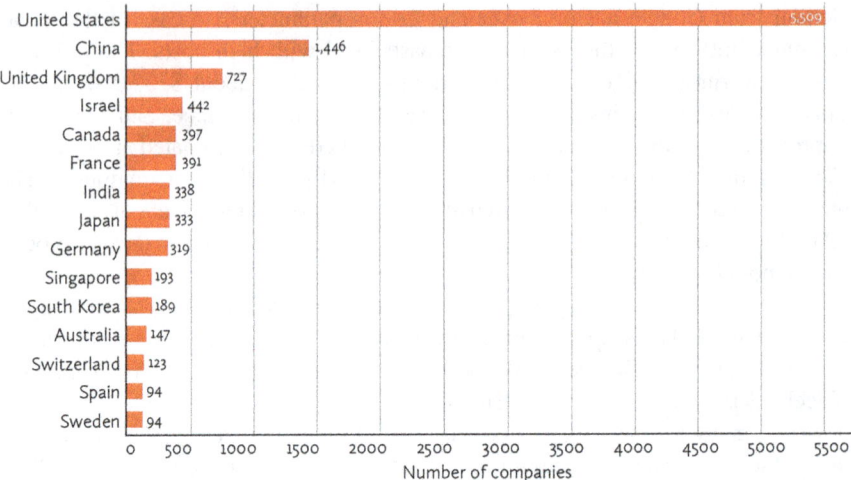

Fig. 2.6 Number of newly funded AI companies by geographic area, 2013–2023 (sum). (Source: Maslej et al., (2024), Graphics © vielseitig.co.at)

academic institutions over time. For the latter, for universities (at least most of them) and other companies as well as smaller countries, this research is almost unaffordable. This not only affects the development costs but also the competition for employees and researchers.

However, this technological boost from AI—it represents a truly new development—has not led and is not leading to a really new corporate landscape. This is not the end of Big Tech. On the contrary, we are seeing its growing dominance. Most new companies have large investments from the dominant IT companies. They are thus protecting themselves in all directions, following Porter's strategy of "competitive response" so as not to miss anything (Porter, 1980).

The final business model, i.e., how companies make money with AI, is still open. At the same time, development is concentrated in a few countries, as Fig. 2.6 shows based on the start-ups from 2013 to 2023. The USA and China dominate. The order of this list also corresponds to that of the countries by the amount of their respective private investments in AI.[48]

Interestingly, however, scientific research, according to the number of scientific publications, is evenly distributed between China, Europe, the USA, and the "rest of the world" (Maslej et al., 2024), so there is no concentration similar to that in the other areas of the innovation chain.

---

[48] Looking at this differently, however, means that Europe and other countries not only have to catch up in terms of investment, but they also have to invest more in proportion.

Regarding the global division of labor in AI, authors such as Crawford (2021) or Tubaro et al. (2020) point to a large digital divide and the danger of a "re-colonialization" with a "new" geography of data production: Not only are the systems for the Global South largely built without their data (see explanations on bias), their natural resources such as the rare minerals necessary for the IT industry are exploited, and they also provide the cheap labor for machine learning.[49]

Munn (2024) uses ChatGPT as a case study for these problems. The company encountered the problem during the development that it regularly delivered racist, sexist, and other toxic responses. The solution: a company with a branch in Kenya with its Kenyan employees trained an AI using provided examples of violence, hate speech, and sexual abuse to classify and filter such texts. The employees had to read and manually label all these texts. These people are thus doing the dirty work of the clean digital world; for 1.30–2 dollars per hour. This shows very well how the labor force of the Global South "serves" the Global North, in this specific case the wealthy companies located there.

Anthropomorphism: AI Like a Human?

We tend to attribute humanlike characteristics to machines. We project ourselves into this device and thereby elevate it. This makes it quasi-"demachinized" and then "humanized." This anthropomorphism is also evident in our descriptions of AI, and this is also used consciously. It is not just a machine; it is intelligent, and it learns and answers questions, all things that only humans do and that should be reserved for humans.[50] This is used in design to achieve better acceptance by humans. Figure 2.7 shows a robot that was deliberately designed for these purposes with warm facial and eye features (large and round).

It seems that we, humans, make the machine special, and perhaps this is the core of the problem of our relationship with machines that can solve complex tasks for us.

There is a long history showing that users react socially to machines, but systems that improve personal empowerment through direct manipulation principles—where the application is predictable and controllable—have been more (commercially) successful. An example can be early ATMs, which started with anthropomorphic designs. These disappeared in favor of direct manipulation and informal neutral address. For example, ATMs communicated with the following phrases:

---

[49] https://time.com/6247678/openai-chatgpt-kenya-workers/; https://www.wsj.com/articles/chatgpt-openai-content-abusive-sexually-explicit-harassment-kenya-workers-on-human--workers-cf191483.

[50] See also the criticism of this by Jaron Lanier, one of the pioneers of computer science (https://www.newyorker.com/science/annals-of-artificial-intelligence/how-to-picture-ai).

Fig. 2.7 A friendly robot. (Generative AI, Adobe Stock, file number: 801129404 © Anasaiimages, Adobe Stock)

1. "I can help you determine your account balance, get cash, or make a deposit."
2. "You can determine your account balance, get cash, or make a deposit."
3. "Account balance, cash, or deposit?"

Quasi as a rule, the third—compact—form prevails.[51]

A historical example of human projection was provided in the 1960s by the German American AI researcher Joseph Weizenbaum, who emigrated to the USA in 1936, with his program ELIZA (Weizenbaum, 1966).[52] ELIZA (see Fig. 2.8) simulated an automatic psychotherapy, with only a few hundred lines of code. The logic of the program was simple, far from the complexity of psychoanalysis, but users attributed the abilities of a psychotherapist to it and interacted seriously with the computer. The communication behavior toward the program corresponded to that toward a human conversation partner. It was not important whether the respondent at the other end of the line was really a human or a computer program. It only mattered that the answers appeared "human." Some believed that the computer would really understand the problems—a phenomenon that has since been called the ELIZA effect. The program was intended as a critique of the anthropomorphization of computers and the overestimation of its abilities. However, Weizenbaum found, based on the reactions to his program, that it was massively

---

[51] Mailing list Google Groups "Human-Centered-AI", operated by B. Shneiderman, August 8, 2024.

[52] The interdisciplinary AI research center Weizenbaum Institute, in Berlin, funded with many millions, is also named after him. This is similar to the UK, where there is the publicly funded Alan Turing Institute. One would expect Austria to pay homage to one of its greatest scientists, the logician Kurt Gödel, with an institute. This is not the case, although Austria is proud of its great historical role in science.

Anthropomorphism: AI Like a Human?

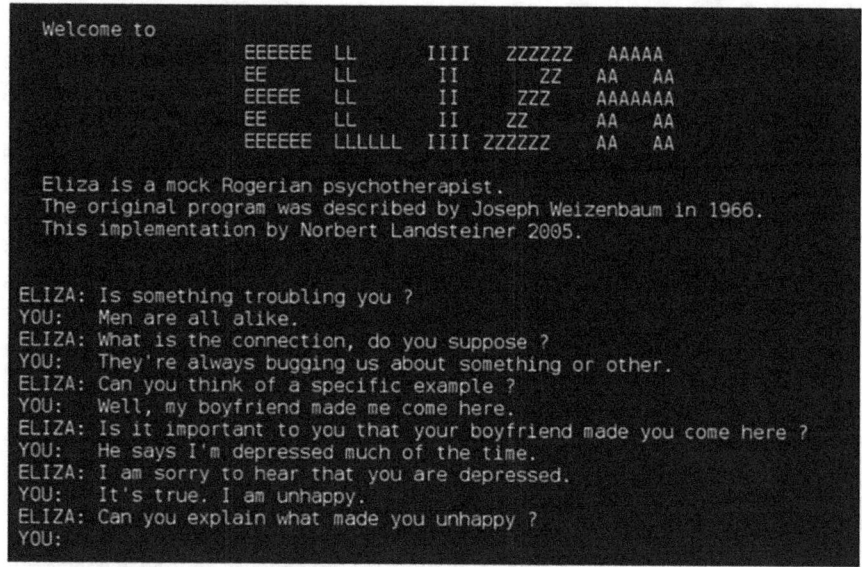

Fig. 2.8 Screenshot of Weizenbaum's ELIZA—"Automatic person-centered psychotherapy". (Source: https://de.wikipedia.org/wiki/ELIZA © public domain)

overestimated and even psychotherapists believed in the possibility of a computerized psychotherapy.

But history seems to repeat itself, which also seems to shed light on the difficulties of our human communication. As so often, such software tools reveal our human problems. If we are tired of people and communicating with them, there are now bots like SocialAI that take over. Here, as with EILZA, you know that you are communicating with a machine/AI. In addition, unlike before, you can now also choose the "character" (e.g., optimist or pessimist) of your artificial counterpart. Another similar example of simulating human communication is NotebookLM from Google with its ability to generate an oral conversation between two people from written text. This can then be used in a podcast. Here, too, you know that this is the machine doing it. While listening to the conversation (which is structured according to simple rules), you are tempted to forget this. What would Weizenbaum say?[53]

---

[53] However, it is known that Noam Chomsky is very critical of LLMs; see, for example, https://chomsky.info/20230424-2/. Noam Chomsky is a renowned linguist, philosopher, cognitive scientist, and political activist, widely regarded for his groundbreaking work in linguistics and critical analysis of politics and media.

Are We Demanding Too Much of the Machine?

But the question also arises whether our expectations are not too high when we expect 100% correct answers and decisions strictly according to the rules of a rational, step-by-step process. Herbert Simon (1976) already pointed out the limitations of humans in the decision-making process with the concept of "Bounded Rationality": The rationality in decisions of individuals is limited, and one makes a satisfactory rather than an optimal decision under the given restrictions. Restrictions are, for example, the difficulty of the problem to be decided, the cognitive abilities of the brain, and the time available for the decision (Campitelli & Gobet, 2010). We humans do not conduct a complete analysis of the problem—this is usually not possible—and usually cannot evaluate all possible outcomes a priori to find an optimal decision but choose an option that appears "appropriate." So we humans now demand something from the machine that we ourselves cannot do and are then extremely critical when these expectations are not met.

In addition, Kahneman (2011) has shown that we often decide intuitively ("his" System 1 of fast, unconscious decision-making), and this is in many cases necessary but often also necessarily wrong. Not only the machine is limited but also the human, as we also know—just look at the state of the world. And we often find explanations in retrospect: a study of Israeli judges hearing parole cases found a high correlation between denial of parole and the time since the last lunch break. However, the judges interviewed afterward all said that their decisions were always "correct" and in line with the criteria (Danziger et al., 2011). So one could only hope to get a hearing date after lunch.

AI: A Preliminary Balance

I will provide my brief personal assessment of the current AI situation, where we, however, should be aware of the so-called Amara Law.[54] It states that we tend to overestimate the impact of a technology in the short term and underestimate it in the long term. Given this background and in particular the extremely rapid development, any assessment is provisional. AI can currently point to undeniable, almost spectacular successes, far beyond expectations. It is advancing into areas that were previously reserved for humans. This of course also raises great economic expectations. However, there is also list of problematic points that should also be mentioned in such an assessment:

---

[54] Named after the American futurist Roy Amara (1925–2007), former president of the Institute for the Future.

- Current AI systems are story machines (however, with consistent stories). They are not bound to facts or the "truth." They also enable conscious manipulation through misinformation and fake news with the associated danger in public discussion: Who can we still trust? But this is true even without AI, if you look at the history of media. So maybe you shouldn't trust anyone 100%.
- Bias: This does not only concern the distortion of the data used to train the systems, because as we have seen, there are different types of bias. For example, the data on the Web is generally distorted, and then there is the question of how the data is selected and on what basis. And every selection of data contains a certain view of the world that the data is supposed to describe. In this respect, these systems also make our prejudices visible. In addition, misclassifications may occur.
- Blackbox: The respective steps leading to the output result are not explainable and comprehensible, even if we knew the code. This raises questions of transparency and accountability. This results in limitations in sensible areas such as justice or medicine. The issues of understandability and explainability are currently probably the most important ones, and they are in the center of AI research.
- This is related with "AI safety," which refers to the field of study and practice dedicated to ensuring that AI systems operate reliably, ethically, and in alignment with human values, minimizing risks such as unintended harm, misuse, or loss of control. Here we need robust system design (with redundancies and error detection) and rigorous testing and validation methods (risk detection before deployment).
- Jobs: The impact of generative AI on jobs and the forecasts for this are currently not consistent and should be viewed with caution. The ILO (International Labor Organization) is also taking a cautious approach here but predicts that high-income groups or so-called knowledge workers (clerical support workers, followed by technicians and associate professionals) will be most affected (Gmyrek et al., 2023). More precise is the PwC AI Jobs Barometer 2024, which shows that industries with high AI usage see a leap in productivity.[55] On the corporate side, a well-known and at the same time not very sympathetic example is the Swedish electronic payment service provider Klarna, which is also repeatedly criticized by consumer advocates. It has not hired any new employees for over a year and is relying on automation through AI.
- In addition, and this is a key issue with AI, we can observe a very high level of economic concentration in development and market penetration. A few companies and countries dominate the field, and there is a risk of dependence and loss of sovereignty, or such a situation already exists. This may also have impact on other sectors, e.g., schools and education. Schools have the problem that, on the one hand, AI tools are already having a massive impact on teaching and, on the other hand, there are not enough materials and staff to teach AI. The authorities are not reacting in time. At the moment, the big IT companies are filling this gap

---

[55] https://www.pwc.at/de/presse/2024/ai-jobs-barometer-2024.

and are providing good teaching materials at low cost (usually free of charge).[56] This is not to criticize the companies; it is rather pointing to an obvious weakness of public school administrations. AI has real potential in this area in particular, as the example of the Khan Academy shows.[57]

- A really critical point is the high energy consumption of the Ki during training and operation. Just think of the data centers required and their cloud solutions. Their energy consumption is often equivalent to that of entire countries such as the Netherlands or Argentina. This also means that even decommissioned coal and nuclear power plants are being reactivated. For example, the decommissioned Three Mile Island nuclear power plant was put back into operation to supply Microsoft data centers, and OpenAI is committed to building huge data centers. And the major IT platforms are currently campaigning for and investing in the construction of new nuclear power plants.
- Military use: The current wars in Ukraine and the Gaza Strip show that the future of warfare is also moving toward artificial intelligence. Ukraine, Russia, and Israel (and not only them) are already using AI on the battlefield (e.g., to identify targets more quickly). Unfortunately, there is now enough training material available, e.g., in Ukraine, where there are millions of hours of footage from drones with which AI models can be trained. And Israel has been building an "AI factory" for war for some time, which is now in use in the Gaza Strip, and this did not necessarily lead to a "clean" war with fewer deaths.[58]
- However, there are also some concerns about possible limits to this development from a technical and data point of view, such as a flattening of the performance curve of LLMs. Another point is that LLMS are hungry for data, where some experts are raising the alarm that "real" data is running out. In addition, more and more companies and institutions are refusing to release their data, at least free of charge. Methods are currently being developed to learn from synthetically generated data. However, it is not at all clear how this affects the quality of LLNs.[59] For example, Shumailov et al. (2024) investigated what happens when LLMs contribute a large proportion of the text found online. They found that the indiscriminate use of "artificial" data during training causes irreversible defects in the resulting models—they call this "model collapse."

---

[56] For example, Google with https://experience-ai.org. One of the few civil society initiatives, on the contrary, is "Digitalization and Us" (in German), by the Vienna City Library. https://www.digital.wienbibliothek.at/urn/urn:nbn:at:AT-WBR-1565583.

[57] https://www.khanacademy.org/.

[58] *Reuters*; Max Hunder (December 20, 2024) and https://www.washingtonpost.com/technology/2024/12/29/ai-israel-war-gaza-idf/.

[59] The *New York Times*; Cade Metz; Tripp Mickle (December 19, 2024).

- In addition, the question of who owns the data and where the copyright lies is unclear: Who is allowed to use what and when? In addition, there are massive data protection problems and the question of how data protection can be guaranteed and controlled.

The sub-symbolic AI has inherent limitations such as lack of everyday knowledge and non-existent ability to abstract. Although it is a powerful tool for language processing and is capable of mapping our language into an immense neural network with billions of parameters incomprehensible to us, we cannot assume that it understands language. It does not "know" what grammar is. The thought experiment called the "Chinese Room" by philosopher John Searle may illustrate this (Searle, 1980): A person who does not speak Chinese sits in a closed room. Through a slot in the wall, he is given questions in Chinese, which he is supposed to answer. He has a manual in his native language and Chinese scripts that contain the information necessary for the answer. The manual contains instructions on which characters he should respond with in reaction to certain characters in the question. The person carries out these instructions purely mechanically, without understanding the meaning, and gives the answer cards through the slot to the outside, without having understood the questions. The people outside assume that there is a Chinese speaker in the room. A seemingly intelligent computer, therefore, does not necessarily have to possess "intelligence" to perform complex tasks.[60]

At the same time, however, AI raises the question of what is human and what is intelligence. If this presupposes that questions outside the respective training data are reliable and can be answered safely and that the system adapts to novel circumstances it has not previously encountered, then these systems are currently very limited. In addition, an AI system at "human level" would have to possess something like consciousness to assess itself and the reactions triggered by its actions and thus also an ethic or a sense of justice. It would also have to have common sense (or machine sense) with a connection to reality and the ability to think abstractly. And here I am wrongly limiting the "intelligence" question to mental "head" characteristics and not considering the physical, emotional, and social dimensions.

Regarding the two classes of AI methods, it should also be noted that a large part of the scientific community points to the possibility of a "neuro-symbolic synthesis," a combination of the logical and the data-driven approach. This would be a way to eliminate the limitations of the latter. This concerns the black box problem and that of missing explainability. It could also ensure "safe" behavior of the AI with the help of formal rules, using the possibility of abstraction and common-sense reasoning. Such a perhaps possible synthesis is currently a hot topic in research.[61]

As previously described, these sub-symbolic AI story machines lead to an interesting reversal in our relationship with the "computer": computers are supposed to

---

[60] For criticism of this experiment, see https://de.wikipedia.org/wiki/Chinesisches_Zimmer#cite_note-1.

[61] See the Digital Humanism workshop "Paradigm Shift in Computer Science?", Nov 2024, TU Wien, https://informatics.tuwien.ac.at/stories/2745/.

solve problems for humans with 100% certainty. We have delegated our problems and can rely on the solutions delivered; the computer is, so to speak, the final authority. These "new" AI systems now sometimes "invent" results, and their truth is not guaranteed. It is now up to us humans to evaluate this truth. The respective tasks in our division of labor with the machine have thus been swapped. In a sense, humans have regained control, and they have been re-empowered. Interestingly, this is now experienced and described as a loss of trust and control, and not as a reappropriation. But as Lee (2022) explains, we may never have been in control; this may have been a fiction.

This is associated with a paradigm shift or glide currently taking place in computer science itself, from deterministic machines with clear and guaranteed solutions to probabilistic models with "uncertain" and often unverifiable statements. This will pose a major challenge, from the self-understanding of informatics to its research and teaching activities.

On the economic side, it must be noticed that the final business model is not yet clear, nor is it clear how money can really be made from it and whether the high investments are worthwhile. There are currently difficulties with the integration into business processes. According to an estimate by the American Census Bureau, in July 2024, only 5% of companies had used AI in the previous 2 weeks. And according to a stock market index compiled by Goldman Sachs, which includes the companies that the bank believes have the greatest potential for a change in their earnings through the introduction of AI due to productivity increases, the share prices of these companies have not performed better than the broader stock market since the end of 2022. However, as already noted, the stock markets in general experienced a boom in 2024, with the major technology companies as the biggest winners. Note that these two facts do not necessarily contradict each other. In addition, macroeconomic data also show no signs of a productivity boost.[62] The latest estimates based on official figures suggest that real output per worker is not growing on average in rich countries.

At the same time, the AI landscape is highly concentrated. For the first time in history, it appears that a radical technical innovation (which I count as AI) may not lead to a qualitatively changed industrial structure—on the contrary, the "old" players, the IT platform companies, seem to be able to expand their dominant position. For academics, it is frightening that universities—as the representative of independent research—play a subordinate role in this area in research. One is almost reminded of US President Eisenhower, who warned in his farewell speech in 1961 about the growing power of the "military-industrial complex" in the USA. This complex of the MIC of the time pales in comparison to the emerging Big Tech complex of today.[63] Perhaps not exaggerating, one can already speak of a new feudal system—that of the tech platform companies.

---

[62] The *Economist*, July 2, 2024.

[63] https://www.politico.com/news/2024/12/10/silicon-valley-takes-over-pentagon-00193576.

The sub-symbolic AI delivers results in many areas that surpass problem solutions based on classical model-based approaches. However, science is also about forming models of the object of investigation in order to make statements about it, to understand it better, and to make explainable predications. This does not apply to this form of AI. It works and solves problems very efficiently, but we have no model and no explanation of the solution.

Against this background of an increasing importance of the large IT companies in research and the triumph of sub-symbolic AI, the provocative question arises: Are we now getting a science without a model and a science without universities? Regarding the first point, there are, however, also positive views on the role of this type of AI in the model-building process. AI hallucinations could help scientists explore ideas they might not have otherwise thought of. For example, David Baker, who shared the 2024 Nobel Prize in Chemistry for his research on proteins, describes this type of AI imagination as central to "creating proteins from scratch."[64]

The role of universities is all about resources, such as computing power (including access to very expensive hardware), data access, and human resources. This gap between universities and Big Tech is why universities (at least some) begin to "drop out of the LLM race" and try to focus their research on what is feasible for them, which requires less computing power and data. And this gap is growing. As for therapy, one can only hope that the public and politicians have become more aware of this issue. One—probably the only—strategy is to share resources between universities, such as the Empire AI Consortium with Columbia, Cornell, Rensselaer Polytechnic Institute, and other universities.[65]

General possible answers to this situation in the public discussion—beyond individual universities—also aim at cooperation; here, there are several alternatives: regulation, combined with national research initiatives, public research collaborations similar to CERN (European Organization for Nuclear Research) in physics, or also international AI commissions similar to the IPCC (Intergovernmental Panel on Climate Change—UN World Climate Council), for assessments of the scientific basis of climate change, its impacts and future risks, as well as possible adaptations. The original idea of an AI moratorium is off the table. Nobody adhered to it, not even those who co-signed.

AI is a very powerful tool, and it is a general-purpose technology that serves as the basis for other technological and thus economic and social developments. The possible applications are diverse and currently not really foreseeable. In addition, it must be recognized that we are already "living" with these machines, and this will intensify. Our decision-making and actions are no longer independent of these machines—for example, without intelligent tools for filtering information, we would drown in the flood of information or perhaps no longer be able to find our

---

[64] The *New York Times*; William J. Broad, December 23, 2024.
[65] Isabelle Bousquette, *Wall Street Journal*. July 12, 2024.

way from A to B. These machines are here and will stay here. It is therefore about the social and "human-appropriate" goals of how this technology is developed and used: to complement and improve our skills or to replace us and our work. Or in other words, our goal should not be for people to do hard work for a minimum wage while robots write poems and paint. This should not be the future.

Chapter 3
Informatics

The basis of this development is the computer and its "science," informatics (or in the Anglo-American context, computer science). Compared to other sciences, it has a very short history. In Austria, for example, the first study programs did not appear until the early 1970s. That's when I started studying, and coincidentally, the Internet was also invented and developed in those years. At the time, however, I had difficulty explaining to my family, friends, and acquaintances what I was doing. Today, 50 years later, computerization has spread to all areas; in 2018, the well-known Swiss Egyptologist Antonio Loprieno (former chairman of the Austrian Science Council) even described informatics as the Latin of today. The computer together with informatics can be described as general-purpose technology (technology that can be used for general purposes—such as AI); its methods, paradigms, and artifacts (hardware and software) are comprehensive and fundamental. Without informatics, the story in this book would not exist, nor would digital humanism. Therefore, I dedicate two major subchapters to it, one on the nature of informatics and one on its history.

The Nature of Informatics

The computer is a "general-purpose automaton" that can control itself through software and can be "instantiated" by software into a specific problem-solving machine, e.g., once into a control device for a power plant or another time into a social media tool. This general automaton has the unique property of being able to change and control its own behavior based on external inputs and internal states—i.e., to react to itself, to act "self-reflectively." The computer is thus able to operate without human intervention, with the exception of initial programming and setups.[1] In other words, it automates and simulates human thinking or aspects of it, which can also be seen in the performance of some AI tools.

Against this background, I use the comprehensive and far-reaching definition of informatics by Turing Prize winner Kristen Nygaard, which dates back to the 1980s: "Informatics is the science that deals with information processes and related phenomena in artifacts, society and nature" (Nygaard, 1986). Informatics is thus not only concerned with a specific machine, the computer; it considers information processes, regardless of where they take place.[2] It rests on three methodological pillars, the respective importance of which for informatics has varied in its short history: mathematics and logic (for the formal theoretical basis), natural science (with the process from the formulation of hypotheses to their verification), and engineering science (from formal modeling of requirements to design and implementation). This methodological breadth shows very good that informatics is inherently interdisciplinary. The discipline has a so-called computational model as a common denominator. This represents the mapping of the solution steps onto a machine, possibly an abstract one, and the implementation into a corresponding algorithm, which can then be converted into written code, the computer program. An algorithm is a finite and unambiguous sequence of instructions or activities that are intended to lead to a specific goal.

In the history of informatics, there have always been two aspects: (1) finding an algorithmic solution to problems—the first electronic computers at IAS in Princeton were already used for weather forecasts; (2) since an algorithm represents the logical, processual aspect of human thinking, the computer also serves to better understand human thinking and human intelligence. Here, consider the Turing test and the implicit definition of human intelligence that comes with it.[3]

Today, informatics is also a powerful tool for other disciplines and for science in general. It can be used in a variety of ways in scientific calculations and simulations and has changed theory and practice in other disciplines. In this context, "Computational Thinking" (Wing, 2006) is particularly worth mentioning, which considers the approach of informatics, computing, as a formal and analyzable process that can also be applied to other sciences. For centuries, scientific and technical achievements (and normal life—think of cooking recipes) offered informal descriptions of how to accomplish a task. Informatics brought rigor and formalism to the description of solutions in the form of algorithms. In doing so, it also recognized

---

[1] This shows how close the definition of AI as found in the EU AI Law comes to almost all computer-based systems.

[2] In contrast, computer science as such is "only" concerned with the computer.

[3] For Turing, see Hodges (1989). Turing was one of the most influential theorists of computer science, after whom the highest award in computer science is also named—the Turing Prize. Turing provided fundamental contributions to AI such as the Turing Test, which is supposed to check whether a machine has thinking equivalent to that of a human. According to Turing, this is the case when a human cannot distinguish the machine from another human in a dialogue (written communication via keyboard and screen).

that not all solutions are equally good. The analysis of algorithms to understand the inherent computational time and memory (= cost) is a great intellectual achievement that also finds wide application beyond informatics.

Conceptually, informatics has brought about a new perspective—see the definition by Nygaard—on natural and human-made phenomena by providing an "informatics" theory with its ontology, epistemology, and methods. It shows two inseparable faces: (1) *Informatics as Subject*, where computer science deals with itself as a science, such as research and development in areas like algorithms, information representation, programming languages or software engineering, etc., and (2) *Informatics in Subject*, as a tool and methodological approach for other sciences and application areas.[4]

This discipline can also be seen as a science of abstraction, with this abstraction, unlike other sciences, materializing in virtual artifacts, i.e., in software. However, system developers and software engineers are far removed from the users. In a kind of technological mediation, the software developers influence and control the users from a great temporal and spatial distance. Peterson et al. (2023) refer to this as an abstracted power ("abstracted power"): "[…] a human actor's influence or control over a system, process, or dataset which […] obscures or distances the human actor from consequences of that influence or control." Thus, an abstraction performed by software can also be seen as an exercise of power by computer scientists, software engineers, and programmers.

In addition, informatics also illustrates well that the separation between basic research and applied research, such as solving concrete problems in ecology, i.e., the use of computer science methods in other disciplines, is difficult. This is also shown by the current developments in AI, about machine learning or the "data-driven computing paradigm": through (1) the combination of an empirical approach (learning from data) with formal methods and algorithms as well as programming and system development and (2) the intertwining of application and research—research in this area lives from real application data and their understanding and interpretation.

Informatics is capable of creating new things, both virtual and real. Just take the rich world of software and hardware, which knows almost no physical limitations. Here it has similarities to art. In addition, its artifacts seem to be both ubiquitous and disappearing, with developments like the Internet of Things. Software is apparently everywhere. Today's somewhat more complex systems consist of a stack or a set of different components, hardware (not just computers but also any other machines—think of traffic systems or individual vehicles) and software, with tasks increasingly being delegated to the software. Software is more flexible. Such parts are easier to replace and therefore also cheaper. This leads to an increasing virtualization. One could almost say that every machine touched by software becomes a computer. Or to put it more pointedly: Does the virtual control the physical?

---

[4] Computer science can be both *emperor* or *plumber*—but the responsibility for this lies not only with computer science.

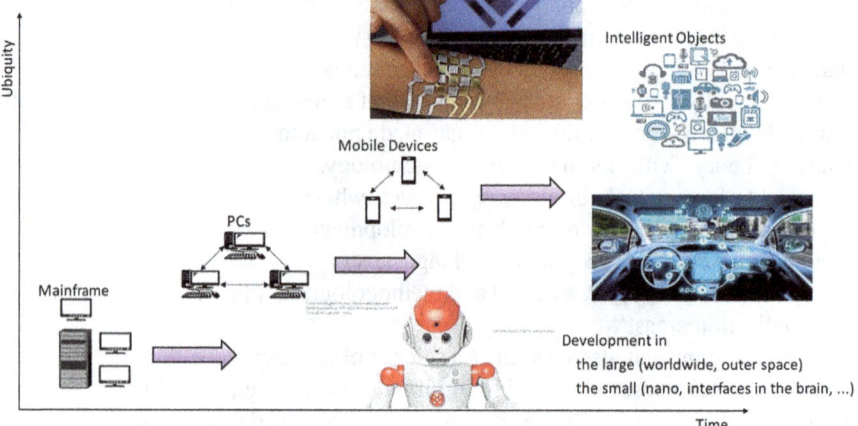

Fig. 3.1 From the mainframe computer to the connected worldwide machine. (Source: Lecture Innovation, TU Wien, 2017 © Hannes Werthner)

We are witnessing a metamorphosis of the computer, from a stand-alone calculator, originally designed to perform calculations, to a global media machine that connects everything and at the same time partially "disappears" into other devices or even into the human body (see Fig. 3.1, with a development from mainframes to networked personal computers and mobile devices to "smart" objects). This machine expands into the almost infinitely large as well as the small. And it is essential for the functioning of our society.

Brief History of Informatics[5]

Table 3.1 briefly summarizes the history of informatics. Its development corresponds to an evolution, because the "results" and artefacts of each phase are found again in the next and do not completely replace them—from the manipulation of numbers in the first electronic calculating machines to the use as a tool in operational application to worldwide networking and the "integration" of individual people and ultimately "all" devices. This also corresponds to an "expansion" in space and function.

In the following sections, I will go into more detail about individual historically important stages of development. This overview cannot, of course, be complete, and is also subjective.

---

[5] This subchapter largely follows Larus (2024), an excellent introduction to informatics and its history.

Table 3.1 From numbers to a device and medium for everyone and everything

Time period (approximately)	Technology	Scope/Goal	User base
1945–1955	Early electronic computers	Calculation	Single user
1955–1975	Mainframes, databases	Information processing in companies	Time sharing, multiple users simultaneously
1970–1990	Hosts and networks, communication protocols, personal computers	Communication between companies and organizations. Home computer/private computing	Multi-user, private
1990–2010	Distributed systems, multimedia, worldwide networks	Communication with private individuals, distributed computing	Everyone
2005–	Mobile, smart/embedded, IoT[a], Cloud	Pervasive and ubiquitous	Everyone and everything

Source: Lecture E-Commerce, TU Wien, 2014 © Hannes Werthner

[a] *IoT* Internet of Things, where every device can receive an Internet address and thus be integrated into the worldwide network

The Beginning: The Electronic Computer

One can start this story with Turing and his machine.[6] This concept of a universal machine was developed by Alan Turing, an English logician, to clarify one of the fundamental questions of mathematics: He showed that there is no general method to decide whether a mathematical proposition is true or false (Turing, 1936).[7] For this, he developed the so-called Turing machine, which only exists as a theoretical model. This machine was abstractly capable of executing any arbitrary algorithm. Turing treated instructions for control (the program) as data. Thus, he created the concept of the "Stored Program Computer." Programs turn computers into universal machines.

As you can see, the origins of computer science were also the search for computability and secure statements. The world was to be represented in formal statements

---

[6] Actually, this is not totally true. One could also start with a more engineering-heavy beginning, and there is a long history before Turing going back to antiquity (see Haigh & Ceruzzi, 2021; O'Regan, 2021; or also Reichl, 2024).

[7] This is the so-called decision problem. Turing dealt in particular with the halting problem—this is a decision problem that deals with the question of whether a certain computer program, given an input, ever stops its execution. Alan Turing demonstrated the undecidability of this question. Another "giant" of logic was the Austrian Kurt Gödel with his incompleteness theorem (1931), which shows the limits of formal systems. He proves that in sufficiently strong systems (e.g., arithmetic), there must be formal statements that can neither be formally proven nor refuted. This sets a fundamental limit to mathematics—and therefore also to computer science "as coded mathematics."

and then in programs. This made it possible to prove the statements, and with Turing, the computability of programs should then be used to say something about the world.

However, a Turing machine was a mathematical abstraction, not a real physical computer. The first electronic computers were built a little later, during World War II. In Great Britain, this was the Colossus based on electron tubes; it helped solve problems like decrypting German submarine intelligence codes. So then Turing played a central role in the British efforts to crack the German Enigma codes in Bletchley Park (For criticism of this experiment see https://de.wikipedia.org/wiki/Chinesisches_Zimmer#cite_note-1).[73]

In the USA, the first electronic computers were developed for calculating the trajectory of artillery shells and later used in the development of the hydrogen bomb. These early computers were already electronic and not mechanical like their immediate predecessors. Figure 3.2 shows the ENIAC, the first electronic computer in the USA.

Shortly after the end of World War II, the Hungarian-American mathematician John von Neumann, building on the work of many others, combined theoretical insights with practical technology. He described an architecture for memory-programmable computers, which laid the foundation for the modern computer industry. This "Von Neumann architecture" is still found in modern computers (Fig. 3.3), with a memory, a control unit, an arithmetic-logic unit (ALU), input, and output. The form, design, and implementation of such architectures have changed

Fig. 3.2 ENIAC, the first electronic computer in the USA. Glen Beck (Background) and Betty Snyder (Foreground) program the ENIAC. (Source: https://en.wikipedia.org/wiki/ENIAC ©public domain)

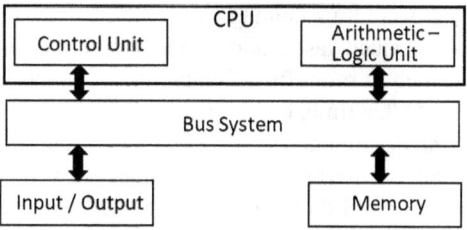

Fig. 3.3 John von Neumann computer architecture. (Own drawing)

over time, but their fundamental operation remains almost unchanged. Interestingly, as early as 1834, the Englishman Charles Babbage designed a similar model of a computer with his analytical engine (which was never built).[8]

The computer architecture has a great similarity with the structure of a company: The control unit orchestrates the work and interprets the computer program step by step. It corresponds to the management of a company. The arithmetic-logic unit (ALU) is doing the work. It executes the individual program commands, like the workers in a company. The memory contains the data to be processed—corresponds in a company to the warehouse with its products to be processed. The input of data and the output of results correspond to the purchasing and sales departments of the company. In Fig. 3.3, the ALU and control unit are combined into the so-called central processing unit (CPU). The bus system is used for internal data exchange. It corresponds to the internal communication of a company. As you can see, Babbage was also active as an organizational consultant for companies during his long career. The trick with computers is that both programs and data are stored together in memory and are only "treated" differently when they are executed. This makes the computer a universal machine.

The first computers were, as also partially visible in Fig. 3.2, programmed by women. The first "computer program" in the 1840s also came from a woman, Lady Ada Lovelace, daughter of Lord Byron. She was also the first to realize that Babbage's analytical engine could be used for more than just computing. In one of her "Notes" to Babbage, she wrote instructions, which many consider to be the first computer program. It is a sad part of the history of informatics that women lost this role over time.

The Computer as a Calculator

In the beginning, computers were used as calculators, to make mathematical calculations. They were expensive and slow, with very limited functionality, and they had a focus on operational applications at that time. For example, IBM rented its 701 computers for $15,000 per month for an 8-hour workday (converted to today, $169,000 USD). These computers could perform about 16,000 additions per second

---

[8] It is unclear whether von Neumann knew of Babbage's work, but this is suspected.

and were thus unimaginably slower than modern devices. On the other hand, they were much faster and more reliable than the then available common alternative, namely, a room full of employees with mechanical calculators.

At that time, building a computer was a major challenge, as was the task of convincing companies to buy. The computer industry started slowly, only to grow faster later. Similarly, the societal impacts or those on the workplace were minor. Only over time did computers replace the job market for human "computing servants"; these were usually women who performed calculations by hand or with mechanical calculators.

At the academic level, on the other hand, there was great intellectual excitement about the potential of this new machine, then also called "Thinking Machine."[9] During this time, Turing also posed the question with his Turing test whether such a machine can think (Turing, 1950). During the test, a person would have a written dialogue with both a human and a machine without knowing who is who. If the examiner cannot reliably tell them apart, the machine is deemed to have passed. Now, 70 years later, this question can now be asked anew with ChatGPT.

Informatics as the Science of Computation and Computability

In the 1960s and 1970s, informatics developed into an independent academic discipline. In addition to the questions of computer construction and its programming or the development of programming languages, people dealt with the question of what is solvable or computable. Turing had already shown that computers, despite their property as universal "computing machines," cannot solve every problem. In the 1960s, this was expanded by also considering the effort and costs (e.g., runtime of programs), something that is not irrelevant when solving real problems. People began to analyze the runtime of algorithms and, if possible, to look for more efficient problem solutions. It quickly became clear that for many basic problems, for example, sorting a list of numbers, there are many solutions (= algorithms) that differ in their runtime. Of course, the faster and more efficient ones were then used. Computer science is therefore also a guild of efficiency, in addition to one of effectiveness.

With this, it was also recognized that problems could be classified according to the runtime of their solution algorithms: Many problems could be practically solved by algorithms whose running time only increased slowly as the amount of data increased; for other problems, however, there was no other solution than to examine an exponentially growing number of possible answers.[10] This class of problems

---

[9] What a reference to today.

[10] Such as the problem of the traveling salesman, who must find the shortest route between x cities but can only visit each city once (except for the first city). There is no procedural solution here. One must essentially consider all alternatives. The first group of problems, whose runtime increases slowly, is called P and the second group NP.

could and can only be solved precisely for small instances. Once again, one can see that at the core of computer science is the question of what is formally computable and solvable, i.e., has exact solutions and how efficient these are.

Development of Hardware and Its Laws[11]

Informatics benefited from an extraordinary improvement on the hardware side with the silicon semiconductor, the fundamental technology for building computers. The first computers were initially made of mechanical relays, which were later replaced by vacuum tubes that were large, hot, and unreliable. In the 1960s, transistors followed, which were much smaller and also more reliable. Equally important was that many transistors could be packed onto a small piece of silicon, a so-called chip, and wired together. This led to steady size, speed, and also cost advantages.

In 1965, Gordon Moore, co-founder of Intel, observed that the number of transistors on a chip doubled every year. This was later called "Moore's Law." This geometric capacity increase continued for four decades, albeit at a slower pace. A decade after Moore, Robert Dennard published the Dennard scaling law for integrated circuits named after him. He explained how the smaller, more densely packed transistors resulting from Moore's law can also work faster without consuming more power.

Figure 3.4 illustrates this enormous development over three decades on a logarithmic scale. However, from 2005 onward, the speed curve (lower line) stagnated because it was no longer possible due to physical limitations to further increase the speed of computers even though the number of transistors on a chip continued to double. As a consequence of this enormous development from the 1970s onward, the cost of computers dropped rapidly, while at the same time their performance increased. This also accelerated the development of the software industry and led to ever greater applications of computers.

The Personal Computer

This rapid technical development in the 1970s led to the "Computer on a Chip," where all components found space on a single piece of silicon. This quickly transformed the computer from an expensive, difficult-to-build device into a small, inexpensive consumer item that was versatile. And microprocessors made it economically possible to build a "personal" computer (PC) that was small and cheap enough that "everyone" could use it as their personal device, for writing and editing documents;

---

[11] These are not laws in the strict scientific sense as eternally valid statements or in the legal sense as behavioral instructions defined by humans, but empirical observations.

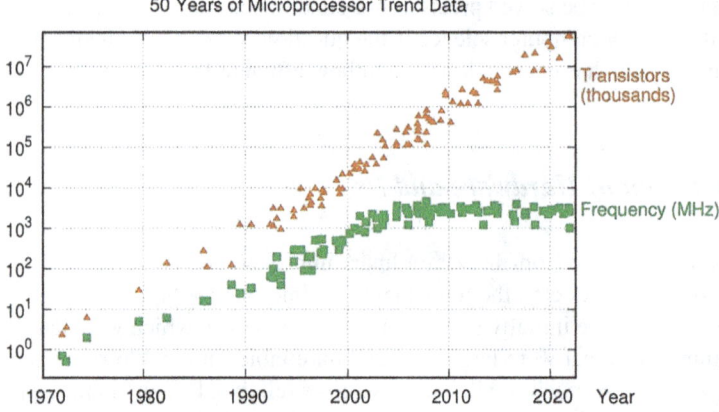

Fig. 3.4 Laws of Moore and Dennard scaling. The number of transistors on a chip has doubled every 2 years for the past 50 years. In the first half of this period, the speed also doubled with each chip generation. As the graph shows (lower line), these speed improvements ended around 2005. (Source: Evolution of Computing; https://www.researchgate.net/figure/Moores-law-and-Dennard-scalingThe-number-of-transistors-on-a-chip-has-doubled-every_fig2_376715484. © Karl Rupp, CC BY 4.0)

for exchanging messages; for writing and executing software; for playing and also for developing new, innovative applications; and thus also for new companies and products and therefore to a new market.

This was also the time of the "Home Computer," often also for "do it yourself" (DIY). Cheap computers like Atari, Amiga, or Commodore—often connected to the TV as an output device and to the cassette recorder as external storage—made it easy to program at home (in the easy-to-learn programming language Basic) and to play. Now, with the rapidly growing number of computers, software also became a profitable, independent business, surpassing computer hardware in creativity and innovation. Before the microprocessor, software was the less profitable appendage of hardware, which was seen by the computer companies as their main product and source of income seen. Bill Gates, one of the co-founders of Microsoft, was one of the first to recognize the revenue source software—and this as an independent business. The value slowly shifted from the hardware to the software.

IBM, the largest computer company of this time, accelerated this process by developing its legendary PC with standard components (a processor from Intel and an operating system from Microsoft) and did not prevent other companies from building "IBM-compatible" computers.[12] IBM created with its "own" PC an open platform that other companies could participate in and benefit from. Many companies emerged that built compatible PCs so that consumers had a wide choice, and prices fell. This in turn promoted the emerging software industry. It is an irony of

---

[12] IBM made the misjudgment that there was no real business to be made with these "small" computers; this was only possible with the large mainframes.

history that in the long term, IBM benefited less from this than other participants like Microsoft or Intel and that IBM's economic importance did not grow with the introduction of its PC but declined.

And the proliferation of powerful personal computers also created a new market segment: the "end users" were born, a technically savvy and growing group of the population, mostly younger people. This then laid the foundation for the next major technological turning point, the Internet and the Web.

Another, probably equally important development started here: Silicon Valley in northern California as an innovation cluster, around leading universities such as Stanford and Berkeley, and many so-called garage companies were founded around these new Silicon-based computers. In the 1970s, the necessary venture capital for investments became an attraction. Everything was possible—also due to fewer or no regulations at all. The name today also stands as a synonym for the "Move fast and break things" principle and thus for free technological "wild west capitalism."[13]

From Text to Graphic: "Natural Interfaces"

Interaction with early computers took place in text form, first via punch cards and later with keyboard and screen. In the late 1960s and 1970s, new graphical user interfaces (GUIs) were developed, especially at Xerox PARC in the USA. With the introduction of the Apple Macintosh computer in the early 1980s, this new form of interaction became widespread. These interfaces used pictorial symbols oriented toward familiar metaphors (such as a trash can for throwing away = deleting), which could be manipulated directly with the mouse and mouse clicks. This made computers easy to use and more accessible to humans. With this graphical user interface, images could be displayed and edited directly. Computers then also used other human interaction mechanisms such as speech recognition and speech generation.

In addition to "stand-alone" computers such as PCs with their "own" user interface, computers are increasingly being integrated into other devices. There they control or interact by means of their functions and properties, for example, in cars or cameras. Mark Weiser called this "ubiquitous computing" (Weiser, 1991): The computer as such recedes into the background, and you are no longer aware of its presence, but it is available anytime, anywhere, seamlessly, and wirelessly.

---

[13] A thorough discussion of the topic would go far beyond the scope of this book. In addition to any "ideological" criticism, one should also point out the concrete problems such as the miserable traffic situation or the extremely high cost of living.

The Internet and the Web

The Internet can be seen as a huge collection of computer networks that are interconnected. It is a network of networks. The term simultaneously denotes the technical infrastructure (the network and the computers connected to it), the data exchange or communication protocol, and sometimes also the entire content of all connected computers, and all people working with them and interacting with each other. Technically, it is a distributed architecture, so there is no central node; the data to be exchanged (ultimately everything is converted into digital data) can move from one computer to another via different routes in this worldwide network. This is comparable to a car driving from A to B in a widely branched road network. It also has several routes available. The failure or breakdown of one or more computers does not lead to the failure of the entire network. It is resilient.

The Internet started as a research project of the US government in the 1970s.[14] Access was initially limited to the military, universities, and a few government-related institutions and companies. In the early 1990s, the National Science Foundation (NSF) of the USA—which managed the public Internet—decided to move from a government-funded government project to a commercial product. In a little-noticed but enormously successful action, it handed over the Internet to the so-called "technical community" that had built it and to the private companies that operate the individual networks that make up today's Internet.

Another revolutionary innovation was the World Wide Web (the "Web"). It became the "killer application" for the Internet. It uses the network and the protocol of the Internet. The result was enormous public interest and financial investments. While working at CERN in Switzerland, Tim Berners-Lee developed a networked hypertext system that he called "World Wide Web (WWW)". With the WWW, multimedia content can be prepared, made available, and exchanged on the net, interactively and worldwide. And with the links included in the Web pages, you can surf from Web page to Web page without noticing that you may have switched to another computer. Like the Internet, the WWW, the Web, today not only refers to the system in the narrower technical sense but also to the amount of its content as well as its rules and regularities.

In 1991, CERN released Berners-Lee's design and his software to the public. A few years later, the University of Illinois' Mosaic browser followed, which made it much more user-friendly to access the various content. The academic community, already familiar with the Internet, quickly jumped on the Web. This began an almost unparalleled spread: in a remarkably short time, companies began to create Web sites, and "normal" people bought PCs to gain access to "cyberspace" or to create their Web site to share and receive information, according to the motto: *Everyone is*

---

[14] In 2024, his 50th birthday was celebrated. Vinton G. Cerf and Robert E. Kahn developed a communication protocol (for data exchange) named TCP in 1973/1974 to connect different types of networks. After further developments in the following years, it then became known as TCP/IP—the basic communication protocol of the Internet.

their own journalist. You could now communicate always and everywhere at almost zero cost. Today, 5.5 billion people use the Internet, which is 68% of the total population.[15] Despite its wide distribution, Fig. 3.5 shows a so-called digital divide. This term refers to the fact that not all people and population groups have the same opportunities to access the Internet. This gap exists not only by regions but also by gender and income. Thus, the Internet and the Web are global and at the same time not.

Mobile Computing

The next radical change in this short history of technical innovations—as a further consequence of Moore's Law—was mobile computing, as computers decreased in size and became more energy efficient and power-saving. They could thus be packaged and branded as smartphones. The decisive moment was the introduction of the iPhone by Apple in 2007 (Isaacson, 2011). It integrated a computer in a paperback format with a touchscreen interface. This eliminated the need for a mouse and keyboard. It also had a continuous connection to the wireless telephone network. For the majority of the world, smartphones are now the most important access to the

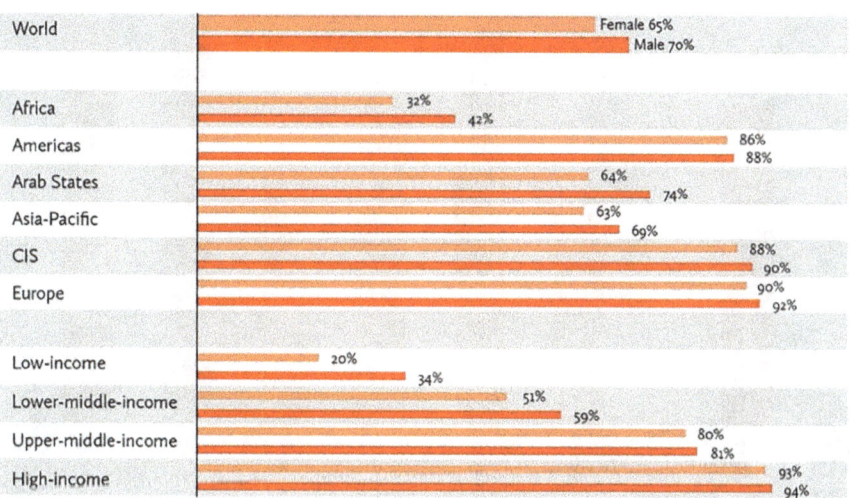

Fig. 3.5 Internet usage worldwide and the digital divide (*CIS* Commonwealth of Independent States, an association of sovereign states, which was founded in 1991 by Russia and 11 other former Soviet republics). (Source: https://www.itu.int/itu-d/reports/statistics/2023/10/10/ff23-the-gender-digital-divide/, International Telecommunication Union (ITU). Graphics © vielseitig.co.at)

---

[15] https://www.itu.int/itu-d/reports/statistics/2024/11/10/ff24-internet-use/.

Internet and the Web. Personal computers, on the other hand, never became smaller than a notebook and are better suited for an office than as a constant companion. In less than a decade, the smartphone has become an object that one (at least most people) always carries with them.

Smartphones also changed and expanded our way of dealing with the "computer." With the integration of cameras and GPS receivers, for example, our personal experience with the world changed. With smartphones, everyone becomes a photographer today, and there is no touristic experience and no visit to another place without this navigational GPS device.

Another consequence of smartphones is that they have made computing more democratic (at least a little), enabled by lower costs, higher availability, and greatly improved, almost intuitive usability. While earlier computers focused on the industrialized countries, smartphones are ubiquitous and are increasingly used in countries of the Global South. But the digital divide remains (see Fig. 3.6). Globally, about 80% of individuals 10 years or older own a mobile phone. Universal ownership (i.e., a penetration rate of over 95%) has been reached in high-income economies. But in low-income economies, only 56% of the population older than 10 years own a mobile phone.

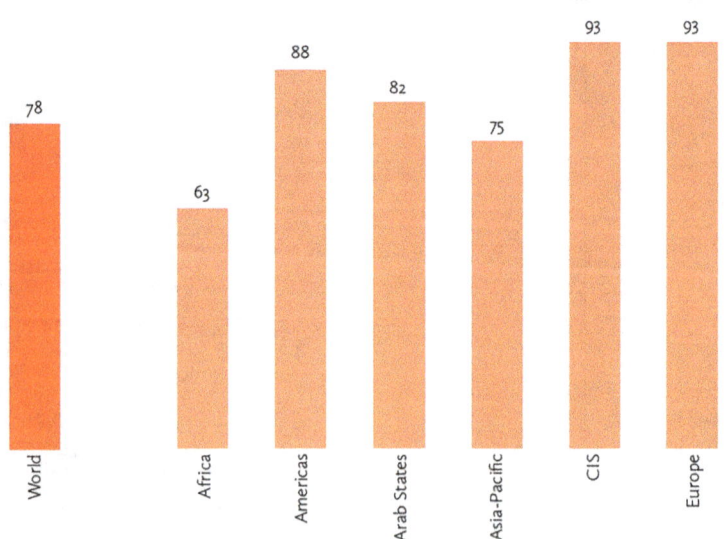

Fig. 3.6 Percentage of individuals owning a mobile phone, 2023. (Source: https://www.itu.int/itu-d/reports/statistics/2023/10/10/ff23-mobilephone-ownership/, International Telecommunication Union (ITU). Graphics © vielseitig.co.at)

Big Data and Cloud Computing

Nowadays, we can capture, store, and analyze enormous amounts of data—"Big Data"—via the Internet/Web. The hardware and software infrastructure for storing and processing this data was originally developed for Web applications such as search engines. These applications use data centers with tens of thousands of computers to index Web pages and make them quickly accessible. Thus, the Web and Web search formed the basis for the development of Big Data.

Internet search was made possible by advances in various areas such as broadband networks, cost-effective storage devices, or the ability to network multiple computers to solve one single task. Amazon was the first company to offer this form of computing and storage, later known as "cloud computing," as a product to others, individuals and companies. In the past, one had to buy and manage their own computers and software. With the cloud, however, they can access scalable systems[16] (hardware and software) via cheap Internet access. This is not only much more cost-efficient but also reduces the administrative effort, making computing increasingly a cheap, convenient, readily available everyday commodity.

This simple collection and storage of data has now led to data being called the "oil" of today, the basic raw material of the new "data economy" with all its far-reaching effects. Without this resource, the next big step in digitalization, AI, would not have been possible. The ability to collect, store, and analyze large amounts of data has also profoundly changed other areas such as science and research. Turing Prize winner and database expert Jim Gray described Big Data as the fourth paradigm of scientific discovery, alongside observation, theory, and modeling (Hey et al., 2009).

---

[16] A system is scalable when it can grow easily without additional or with only minor additional resources.

Chapter 4
The Web

The Internet and the Web can together be considered as the most important technological innovation of today. As described in the previous chapter, this happened very quickly—much faster than with any other technology in the past. This led, in short, to:

- A structural change in the economic landscape with new companies; changed market structures (e.g., online tourism, where online agencies far outperform traditional travel companies); and the simultaneous disappearance of existing industry segments; take, for example, Wikipedia, which has dried up the market for encyclopedias, or the serious problems of the traditional media.
- A social expansion, where, for example, social media platforms or tools like Zoom enable new ways of human communication, especially in times of crisis or over long distances.
- Psychological changes on a personal level with signs of addiction to online communication or—on the positive side—also for personal empowerment through new forms of communication.
- Massive changes on a political and legal level, up to the current geopolitical disputes, as well as the restructuring of the "public" political discourse through social media.
- Even the transformation of our physical spaces, for example, through e-commerce and logistics, and the associated expected decline in the number of physical shopping centers.[1] For example, take Fig. 4.1—the upper picture shows separate paths for smartphone users so that they do not endanger themselves and others when looking at their mobile phones. The lower picture shows traffic light sys-

---

[1] In this respect, the current discussion about soil sealing is not without a certain irony. In a few years, short-sighted politicians and representatives of the profession will blame someone—who—for the increasing sealing.

Fig. 4.1 Upper image: Vilnius, separate paths for smartphone users (picturedesk.com, ID: 20180922_PD17309. © Alexander Welscher/dpa/picturedesk.com). Lower image: Cologne, ground-mounted traffic light system—Fußgängerfurt Aachener Straße/Maarweg (Source: https://de.wikipedia.org/wiki/Bodenampel# © Nicola, CC BY-SA 4.0)

tems installed in the ground so that you can see them when you constantly have your mobile phone in front of you.

The structural changes in the economic sector are illustrated by the e-commerce framework of Fig. 4.2 with the different types of participants such as consumers,[2] companies, markets, and industries up to the societal political framework. Information technology is impacting all the different players and influencing their roles, actions, and strategies, as well as changing all their relationships with each other. A good example of this is again the tourism industry, which has been radically changed by IT. New, now powerful players such as online travel agencies entered the market—and formed their own network-like structures. These new companies

---

[2] We humans are all three at the same time, users, consumers, and citizens.

Fig. 4.2 E-commerce framework. (Source: Lecture E-Commerce, TU Wien, 2014 © Hannes Werthner)

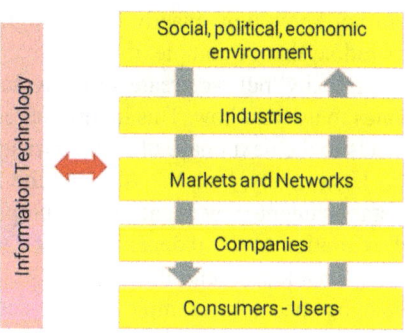

became so powerful that even the legislation had to be adapted (see the numerous court cases against Booking or Airbnb). However, the respective design of IT is also influenced by the individual societal and economic actors, this according to the already mentioned co-evolution.

Entire communication and value chains have thus been "computerized," with the accompanying efficiency increase and acceleration. Speed increased also due to the immediate imitation of business models and technology—Web-based systems are transparent. You can easily see and learn what is behind them. Online services have become "everyday consumer goods" or commodities, and this led to the flexibilization of existing value chains and subsequently to complex network structures (see also Perez, 2002). Just consider today's software development process, where, unlike in the past, code is taken from internally or externally available software libraries and reused. And often these pieces of code are free. Thus, the focus is now *network engineering*, and not *process re-engineering*; thus, the question is: What role do I take in this networked market structure, and what is my contribution? And not so much: How cheap and fast do I do it? Users, as citizens and consumers, were integrated into the communication and market transaction systems, thus leading them through social networks from *customer-focused* to *customer-driven*: Users increasingly get involved, instead of just being served and "examined."

We experience on the Web a simultaneity of constantly new emerging companies and a trend toward concentration (see Chap. 5) with the winner-take-all phenomenon. On a more abstract level, this is a seemingly dialectical development process between order and disorder or, in other words, centralized versus decentralized: constantly new companies (disorder) with simultaneous increased concentration (order). Innovations are essentially driven by IT-based market newcomers. The existing old market participants usually have problems with service innovation, the new business models, and the technical development.

A phenomenon that goes along with this is the so-called transparency paradox: the massively increasing online available information leads simultaneously to both increasing and decreasing transparency. We have "everything" available online, much more than ever before, but how and where do we find this information, or can we trust it when searching? Search and recommendation engines may help, but we do not know how exactly these programs work. This also corresponds to another paradox, that of complexity: We use computers to solve problems, and thus reduce complexity, but we create so many software tools that we no longer know which ones to use and how. This in turn increases the uncertainty and complexity and thus leads to the next phase of computerization to solve problems.

Historically, both the Web and the Internet have their roots also in the US anti-establishment movement and its utopian-cultural vision of the 1970s, e.g., in the Declaration of the Independence of Cyberspace.[3] It foresaw a future with a technically enabled decentralized grassroots democracy with free information exchange in cyberspace, for example, with its news groups or bulletin boards. Key figures like Doug Engelbart envisioned a future in which technology would complement and enhance human abilities, but not replace them. There are still strong elements of such collaborative and participatory approaches, like Wikipedia or the open-source movement, both of which also have large societal and economic impacts.

On a structural level, however, the Web has evolved from a tool for free participatory information exchange without "legal rules" to a highly centralized infrastructure, at the center of which stand a few companies. In areas such as ecology, this phenomenon has already been described as a "tragedy of the commons" (Hardin, 1968). This is a situation in which individuals with unrestricted access to an unregulated central resource cause its destruction through overuse, which contradicts the goal of the common good (for a critical discussion, see also Ostrom, 1990). This phenomenon also applies to the Web. Today's Web essentially follows an advertising-based business model of the classical media with huge search engines and online shops. The model resembles that of newspapers but is expanded by interactivity, personalization, and recommendations (Vardi, 2018). These extensions control how we access which information. News, social media, entertainment, commerce, education, and almost all other information are "tailored" to each user and this in an interactive form. But this goes far beyond traditional media, which also threatens their existence. These new systems are more efficient and interactive, and they improve user experiences. In this huge amount of information, personalization and recommendations are also necessary: They make it possible to find relevant information and products in a vast online landscape. However, personalization and recommendation systems lead to a user behavior that changes over time. The users adapt and increasingly follow the system's recommendations. The basic unit of business is clicks (= user interactions), and one must optimize the number of these clicks to achieve a higher profit for the platform operators. In addition, content was then also negatively emotionalized because it is shown that negative emotions generate more clicks.

This is our contribution to this business model. We users pay with our data. These data describe what we are interested in, what we buy, when we click on what, how long certain content interests us, etc. These systems "read along" so that we can be "served better" next time. We are often not aware of this. On the other hand,

---

[3] John Perry Barlow, *A Declaration of the Independence of Cyberspace*, 1996, https://en.wikipedia.org/wiki/A_Declaration_of_the_Independence_of_Cyberspace.

Fig. 4.3 Our world of selfies and self-referentiality. "Hashtag gold medal athlete smiling for his many gadgets on selfie sticks as he poses for a picture." (Adobe Stock, File number: 92339202 © lazyllama, Adobe Stock)

advertisers pay with real money for our data. They use it for personalized and more effective advertising. But of course, they pass these costs on to the price of the goods and services they offer. So we, the user and consumers, pay twice: through an invisible tax on the products we buy and through our personal data. These data are used in various ways and also sold; companies and also states do this abundantly. This leads then to the surveillance capitalism well described by Zuboff (2019). And we, the users, have become consumers instead of citizens (Stanger, 2020). In the end, in this system, we are users, products (our data), and producers (we produce the data) at the same time; it is almost an economic perpetual motion machine.

On the Web, we seem to have absolute individual freedom, where we can realize ourselves unlimitedly in the virtual, there are almost no rules. But *what I see, what I get*, and *what I do* is defined by the distance measure of the similarity matrix of a recommendation system. This matrix is generated by our interactions on the Web.[4] In addition, there is an algorithmic or statistical relationship between the individual, amplified by our almost narcissistic and excessive self-referentiality (see the parodistic picture of "Selfie Mania" in Fig. 4.3) and the common. This common is calculated from the data and behavior of similar users. Therefore, this common is also a fiction or deception because it is a statistical "summary" of previously

---

[4] A recommender system collects all user signals and interactions. To derive what else might interest us, all—in addition to our past behavior—users with similar behavior are identified to recommend their "content" to us. All of this is stored in a huge matrix.

individualized views. Basically, the conscious decision of what to do is no longer made by humans but by algorithms mostly unknown to us. In the end, we see the promise that everything is possible and there are no limits and that individual freedom and the virtual common are a fiction.

A similar reversal from a social participatory idea to a purely commercial, almost cynical result can also be observed in the so-called sharing economy and the field of influencers. Airbnb may serve as an example. Intended as a way to travel privately and cheaply, where you also—or above all—come into contact with the local population, it is now part of the centralized platform economy (see Chap. 5). It even has a negative impact on local housing markets with increased housing costs and social disruption. This has also led to necessary government regulation. Another example is influencers: at the beginning, they served as honest counter-voices to the exuberant online advertising, but today, they are part of the business, where they are also booked by companies, and it has become their goal to turn the trust placed in them into money.

Under the surface of the "Everything is possible" world, there is a hidden one, with fixed rules and dependencies.[5] Thus, we have the transition from a system that supports individual freedom and democratic participation to a system that is controlled by algorithms. However, it is not the algorithms themselves, it is the interest behind them.

The focus of this development on the Web was obviously on optimization and efficiency, not on sustainability and resilience.[6] Any kind of unproductivity was to be driven out of the system. The goal is an optimized, almost autonomous functioning of the systems, which are also easily scalable. This led to:

- *Informatization and deconstruction of value chains*: Everything is now based on the Internet/Web structure and is optimized by software. Just take the just-in-time production, which is only made possible by this technical infrastructure. This informatization is also a basis of the globalization process and the associated outsourcing of production.
- *Outsourcing*, where we as customers perform unpaid work; think, for example, of e-banking, ATMs, self-check-in, or almost all online services in e-commerce. It is available 24 h a day, possibly worldwide. But at the end, with this customer self-service, we do the work.
- *Privatization*: Our "public" data is now owned by IT companies and used by them. In this context, ChatGPT can also be seen as a data privatization process, where our data is used to train the language models. An interesting example of this private appropriation is the open knowledge platform Wikipedia. It is estimated that almost half of the value of all Google searches is created by Wikipedia content (Vincent & Hecht, 2021; Siddarth et al., 2021).

---

[5] I see digital humanism as a rational response to this individualization and the "Anything goes" paradigm of the Web.

[6] It is almost an irony of this story that the basis of this development, the Internet, was planned and developed with a distributed architecture as a resilient and fault-tolerant system.

Economic Impact

Fig. 4.4 The increasingly dominant role of IT. (Source: Lecture Research Methods in Business Informatics, TU Wien, 2017 © Christian Huemer)

In summary, it can be stated that the Web, in the context of simultaneous legal deregulation in the USA in the 1990s, has developed into a system with the winner-take-all phenomenon. This concentration is also geographically assignable. It is primarily one of the Global North, especially the USA. Estimates suggest that a large proportion of global Internet traffic is routed through the USA (Farrell & Newman, 2019, 2023).[7]

At the same time, these systems of today, with their size and their services, represent a public good that provides services that the public sector cannot provide at that quality. The use of this good is unavoidable, for all of us. However, it is largely in private ownership. This development happened almost unnoticed and is today heavily discussed and criticized.

Economic Impact

The increasing informatization is very well illustrated in Fig. 4.4: IT evolved from "IT supports business" to "IT controls the business" and ultimately to "IT is the business," in the sense that the "laws" of the Web (co-)determine the economic activity of a company (co-determine). This nearly revolutionary development was, however, already recognized and addressed by some in 1988: "More than being helped by computers, companies will live by them, shaping strategy and structure to fit new information technology."[8] This affected and affects all industries and sectors

---

[7] There are divergent views on the exact number (it goes up to 70%).

[8] *Fortune*, Sept. 26, 1988: The winning organization. Referenced in Gurbaxani and Whang (1991).

and the corresponding relationships (see also Fig. 4.2). Examples of this are the traditional print and television media, which, especially in the advertising sector due to their lack of interactivity and personalization as well as their "linearity," have massive disadvantages, or in the field of mobility the European automotive sector, as is now apparent, apparently too late recognized that IT is also a decisive factor in this traditional industrial sector.

Despite the enormous successes, the process of digitalization could not fully meet the expectations placed in it (at least not for everyone). In contrast to the very large promises of the IT industry since the 1980s (this is also the time of the invention of the personal computers and the age of advancing digitalization), income and wealth inequality in practically all large advanced economies have increased (Acemoglu & Restrepo, 2019; Autor, 2014; Piketty, 2021). But not only the gap within society has widened but also the one between companies and between economic sectors. Here, according to the winner-take-all principle of the platform economy, we can observe growing market gaps.

In this context, one must also mention the so-called productivity paradox (see also Brynjolfsson, 1993), so named by Nobel laureate Robert Solow, because although the investments in IT increased, productivity did not increase accordingly. In the 1980s, productivity growth slowed down, when one would actually have expected a significant growth as was also predicted by many. This changed then in the late 1990s, when an increase in productivity at the workplace through the introduction of IT could be observed (especially in the USA). Here, Brynjolfsson and Hitt (1996) diagnosed a significantly positive relationship between IT investments and productivity when these investments were made as a complement to organizational changes, i.e., a non-purely technical approach was chosen, but the entire organization was taken into account.[9] This was already explained by Wigand (1995) who describes the contribution of IT as an indirect one, via improvements of business processes. He argues for an alignment of IT, organization, and strategy to leverage the benefits of digitalization. Overall, however, productivity growth rates have halved since the 1980s, and the share of labor in income has significantly decreased; this has accelerated after the year 2000 (Acemoglu & Restrepo, 2019).

Here, especially the relationship between qualifications of the employees, their work tasks and technology, and the resulting income and employment distribution is complicated. Acemoglu and Autor (2011) analyzed this in the USA and other advanced economies, with interesting results:

1. Significant declines in real wages of low-skilled employees, especially men
2. "Polarization" of wage growth, i.e., simultaneous growth of high and low wages compared to the middle range
3. Increases in employment in highly skilled and low-skilled occupations compared to medium-skilled occupations—called job polarization

---

[9] From the 2000s to the 2020s, productivity growth slowed down in the USA and in industrialized countries additionally; sometimes, this is also referred to as Productivity Paradox 2.0.

4. Rapid spread of new technologies in tasks that were previously performed by moderately qualified employees, with corresponding substitution effects
5. Increasing offshoring of jobs by relocating parts of production to cheaper regions of the world, enabled by information technology[10]

Polarization means that jobs in the middle class—which require a medium level of qualification (employment in medium qualified office, administrative, production, and operational professions such as the jobs of workers in the automotive industry)—are declining compared to jobs at the lower end, which require few qualifications, and jobs at the upper end of society, which require a higher level of qualification. They can be more easily standardized and "automated." The jobs at both "ends," which either involve abstract or non-routine manual tasks, are far less susceptible to this process however. In the first case, capacities such as problem-solving, judgment, and creativity and in the second case flexibility and physical adaptability are required. Since these activities are located at the opposite ends of the professional qualification spectrum—in specialist, management, and technical professions on the one hand and in service and worker professions on the other hand—this can lead to a partial "hollowing out" in the middle. One sees automation and technology have different effects. It depends on the framework conditions and rules.

The search for the causes of this development is difficult; the situation is complex, and the effects are often indirect, diverse, and partly interconnected. But in addition to a neoliberal market ideology with massive deregulation while progressing concentration, technological progress also plays a significant role. Siddarth et al. (2021) notes in the scientific economic community even an increasing consensus that the focus of technological progress on automation and labor replacement is one of the main causes of increasing inequality. Here, there is also no "automatic" correction mechanism. This requires fundamental political reforms and a new form of work organization (Acemoglu & Robinson, 2023).

Efficiency Versus Resilience

During the COVID-19 pandemic, many voices were raised, calling for a fundamental change in our economic system to make it economically, socially, and ecologically sustainable. In the meantime, the crisis is over and apparently forgotten, and business continues as usual.[11] Organizational, technical, and also social resilient

---

[10] With effects on the US election results, essentially in the so-called Rust Belt states. Their former economic prosperity due to steel and automobile production was lost due to technological change and offshoring, with population losses and increasing unemployment.

[11] However, with exceptions: in July 2022, the population in the two Austrian valleys and ski areas Pitztal and Ötztal voted in a referendum (where one might have expected the population to be in favor, as they have economic benefits) against the merger of the two glacier ski areas and further growth.

"architectures" with buffers and fault tolerance, which are not aimed at optimality, were one of the most important lessons. This follows not only from the pandemic but applies especially to the current and much larger energy and environmental crisis, one of the great challenges of our time Vardi, 2024b). We need resilient systems that are capable of adapting to disruptive exogenous variables.[12] Resilience means that the functionality of a system can be maintained under disruptive internal or external influences and that the functioning of a system can be restored as quickly as possible after a disruption.

Our general goal as society, however, was to develop and implement efficient and optimized systems that prevented us from investing in preparation for critical situations. This was pointed out by the well-known columnist Thomas Friedman in the *New York Times* on May 30, 2020:

> *Over the past 20 years, we've been steadily removing man-made and natural buffers, redundancies, regulations and norms that provide resilience and protection when big systems—be they ecological, geopolitical or financial—get stressed [...] We've been recklessly removing these buffers out of an obsession with short-term efficiency and growth, or without thinking at all.*

There are plenty of examples, such as our extremely optimized supply chains, where small disruptions lead to global shutdowns. Therefore, it is currently (politically) being discussed how to better distribute the production of important goods geographically or bring them closer to consumer markets. However, this will lead to additional costs. We will see if this will happen.

Efficiency means achieving optimal results, with the resources provided being used as best as possible, or simpler: Something is efficient if nothing is wasted and everything is optimized. Economically, efficiency means that goods and other factors of production are distributed or assigned to their most valuable uses. Buffers and waste are minimized. Proponents of the free market economy argue that economic efficiency is achieved through individual self-interest and the freedom of production and consumption, thus best fulfilling the interests of society. Looking at the current crisis situations, however, this is not really the case.

Today, everything must be efficient, and no one is allowed to be inefficient. In the digital economy, e-commerce in particular was such an efficiency driver, with the possibility of creating new value in different ways and with little input: (1) for example, added value through simple bundling of existing products and services or also "upgrading"; (2) value extraction by directly reducing costs; through automation, (3) shifting work to customers (e.g., ATMs); or (4) by using customer or sales data for personalization. E-commerce is thus an example of how applications of informatics itself, through the computerization of relationships between companies, organizations, and individuals, laid and continues to lay the foundation for this increase in efficiency. All processes and procedures are optimized. Another example

---

[12] Interestingly, the Internet worked well during the pandemic, because one of its basic principles is redundancy and not optimality, which worked.

are the already described recommender systems—the goal was and is to quickly and efficiently lead users to the relevant information or purchase, and not to ensure a broad, unfocused experience. Interestingly, however, studies also show that with these systems, the goal of short-term optimality, measured as high precision of the recommendation or high CTR (click-through rate)—i.e., you have recommended the "right" thing to the customer, and they take it up quickly—can reduce customer retention in the longer term.

Interestingly, studies also show that with these systems, the goal of short-term optimality, measured as high precision of the recommendation or high CTR (Click-Through-Rate)—i.e., the customer has been recommended the "right" thing, and they quickly take it up—can reduce customer retention and loyalty in the long term.

In addition, informatics itself and its methodology are oriented toward efficiency. In Chap. 3, we saw that algorithms for solving problems are classified according to their resource consumption such as runtime and memory requirements. They are supposed to "guarantee" predictable results with minimal effort. We are looking for the most efficient solutions. Interestingly, one of the most important inventions of informatics, the Internet, was developed according to resilience criteria and principles of fail-safe operation. This has worked well in times of crisis, such as the pandemic but also after the attack on the World Trade Center in New York in 2001. So, it can be done differently.

Digitalization: Cause or Solution

This is one of the important questions: Is IT or digitalization "good," is it the solution to problems with all its achievements, or is it their cause? Very often, IT is seen as the cause, as the culprit. Just think of the current fundamental criticism of social media platforms, including calls for their ban. This question may seem trivial, but the answer is not. Let us look at three examples:

A	Environmental crisis and climate change with rising emissions and energy consumption
−	Currently, the negative side predominates here. Just consider data centers and their cloud solutions: their energy consumption often equals that of entire countries like the Netherlands, especially the training of AI models leading to extremely increasing consumption. And blockchain technology with its cryptocurrencies should actually be banned from an energy standpoint. This leads in both cases to the fact that even decommissioned coal and nuclear power plants are reactivated. Thus, the decommissioned Three Mile Island[13] nuclear power plant was restarted to supply Microsoft data centers, and OpenAI is lobbying for the construction of huge data centers. And the big IT platforms are currently lobbying for the building of new nuclear power plants, and they are investing there

---

[13] In this nuclear power plant in Pennsylvania, USA, there was a partial core meltdown in 1979, where about a third of the reactor core melted.

+	On the positive side are the great possibilities and the potential for increasing energy efficiency; the rapid, comprehensive, and cost-effective collection and processing of information for forecasting or rapid intervention; or the intelligent control of machines, optimized for minimal energy consumption, as well as diverse, new forms of work enabled by IT applications, such as reduced traffic as a result of home office or video conferences. This has proven to be possible during the corona pandemic. In addition, research is very active in this area, so significant improvements can be expected
?	However, if we take a closer look at the situation, we see a direct correlation of the critical environmental situation with our focus on economic optimization and profit in business. This is done under the assumption that short-term profit, according to the theory of the free market, automatically leads to energy-efficient systems (given appropriate incentives) But the current situation shows the already obvious need for truly corrective market interventions. IT could play a supporting role in this
B	**Threat to democracy through the current development, especially in the area of social media—the global democracy index has been declining for 16 years (Metakides, 2024)**
−	Social media—based on recommender algorithms—lead to rapid spread of fake news and filter bubbles as well as a coarsening of language (especially due to the tendency toward negative emotionalization). This has implications for political discussion and the ability to influence elections through so-called bot farms. For example, there is some evidence that the 2016 US elections were influenced by digital disinformation. Another example is the ownership of Twitter/X by Elon Musk and his rather aggressive and one-sided behavior on "his" platform. This is currently hotly debated[14]
+	However, social media platforms also play an important role in the organization of civil resistance, particularly important in authoritarian states. Examples are the democracy movement in Hong Kong or the "Sardine Movement" against the right-wing Lega Nord and their "leader" Salvini in Italy or their role in the successful political protests, especially by young people, in Kenya, Nigeria, and Indonesia in 2024. The imprisoned candidate Imran Khan, for example, interfered in the Pakistani election campaign in 2024 with fake videos. Social media thus also serve as a means for direct participation, for the exchange of free information. This is especially the case in authoritarian states. Further examples from Africa: (a) #Tajamuka as a Zimbabwean online and offline movement for eco-social behavior and government accountability. It was mainly active on X and was so widely spread that the government shut down the Internet. (b) #Feesmustfall was founded by university students in South Africa against tuition fee increases. As a result of the movement, more students of color are now enrolled at South African universities[15]
?	Is the question of democracy not rather an expression of increasing polarization, to which the traditional media (in partly mutually reinforcing interaction with electronic media) also contribute and which is primarily caused by an increasing division of society as a result of growing economic and social inequality? Maybe social media are also used to name someone to blame and to avoid addressing the "real" causes

---

[14] I am not discussing here the effects of IT tools (besides, e.g., social media, e-mail) on human language, for example, through abbreviations, use of graphic symbols, etc. This would go beyond the scope of this book.

[15] https://www.europarl.europa.eu/doceo/document/B-8-2017-0200_EN.html; https://twitter.com/FeesMustFall. Thanks to IWM Junior Fellow Tendai Ganduri for these examples.

C	**Increasing inequality—for example, the richest 10% of the world's population own more than half of the private wealth Piketty, 2021)**
−	As previously stated, automation, under the given political framework conditions and economic objectives, does indeed contribute to the falling wage share of total income since the 1970s/1980s. And it plays a role in the described job polarization and a partial deindustrialization in some regions of the world. When one refers to increasing economic inequality, one also has to mention high percentage of IT company shareholders among the billionaires
+	On the other hand, IT is essential for the functioning of the world and its economic and also social development. Important societal and economically positive developments as well as the global growth with generally increased living standards would not have been possible without IT and technology in general (see also Fig. 1.3)
?	But isn't the economically diverging society rather the result of the neoliberal economic policy prevailing in the last 40 years with simultaneous deregulations (Piketty, 2021)? A lesson from the history of the industrial revolution is that societal prosperity does not automatically occur; fundamental political reforms, a new work organization, and the associated alignment of technology are important[16]

I see IT not as the underlying cause—it enables things and processes but can also significantly amplify them, both positively and negatively. A particularly bad example with regard to social media was pointed out by (Vardi, 2024a, b): in 2022, Amnesty International accused Facebook's parent company Meta of "materially contributing to" human rights violations against the Rohingya in Myanmar. It was argued that Facebook's algorithms "proactively amplify" anti-Rohingya content. The Rohingya conflict has led to mass migration of Rohingya from Myanmar starting in 2015 and to several massacres of Rohingya by the Myanmar army and armed locals in 2017.

On the other hand, IT alone is not the solution either. But we also need to be aware that these systems as such are not neutral; their design, creation, development, and use are based on the objectives of an individual, a company, or society. The focus of research and development and the focus of application are important. It is therefore necessary to "get involved" early on in the life cycle of a technology and its development and application.[17]

---

[16] Acemoglu and Johnson (2023) describe very well that in the first phase of the industrial revolution, there were stagnant wages and worse working conditions. This only changed through social and political change.

[17] All of this seems logical, and one can wonder how often this is not recognized.

Chapter 5
Platforms

If we take a brief look at the development of the "digitalization" business landscape with the most important IT companies, this is a story of only 25 years:

- Google, founded 1998
- YouTube, 2005
- Skype, 2003
- eBay, 1997
- Twitter, 2006
- Facebook, 2004
- Uber, 2009
- Airbnb, 2008
- Instagram, 2010
- Alibaba, 1999
- Tencent, 1998

All these companies are so-called platform companies. Their "value" lies in their network of users and information from/about them as well as about the market. It does not lie in the infrastructure (with the exception of the cloud infrastructure for cloud solutions). Interestingly, all of these companies are newcomers that brought in fundamental innovations in terms of technology and business model from outside. The platform economy touches all economic and societal areas with its new technical services. A platform enables so-called "value-creating" interactions between external providers and consumers (individuals and/or companies). It is a virtual place where providers and consumers meet. The platform provides a technology and service for a broader, "open" "ecosystem." It thus offers an open, participatory infrastructure, with established governance rules (Parker et al., 2016). The goal is to "bring together" different types of users and facilitate the exchange of goods, services, and social "currency" between these users, with a value added for all participants. Based on a common technical-organizational architecture, these platforms are a kind of dialectical relationship between cooperation and competition and centralization around the platform operators who create and control these structures. From a market transactional point of view, they represent a middle ground between an open network structure and a hierarchy, since control lies in the hands of the platform owner. This structure is quite dynamic, as can be seen in Fig. 5.1, with the development from a simple relationship to a complex network of relationships—in our example, the social network for professionals LinkedIn—with a variety of different participants. This makes the "richness" of the evolving network apparent as well as the associated business opportunities. It is about information; physical goods usually play no role.

The development toward intermediaries and further toward powerful central nodes (hubs) in a network structure results from the limits of direct communication between many network participants and the resulting increase in search costs on both sides, supply and demand. An intermediary provides support in the different phases of a transaction between two parties when matching supply and demand: information search, negotiation, settlement of a transaction, and after-sales activities. It gives confidence in the event of incomplete information and the associated

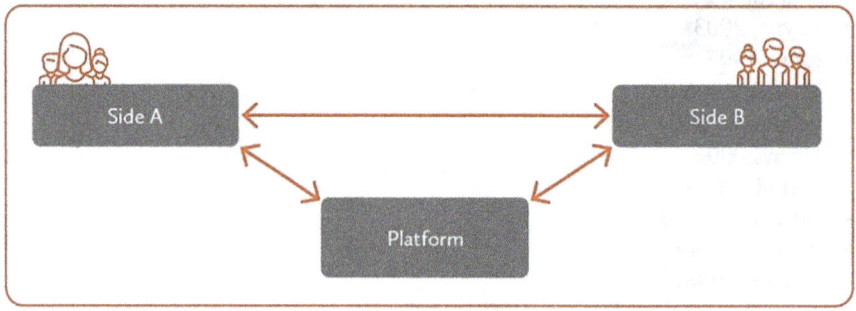

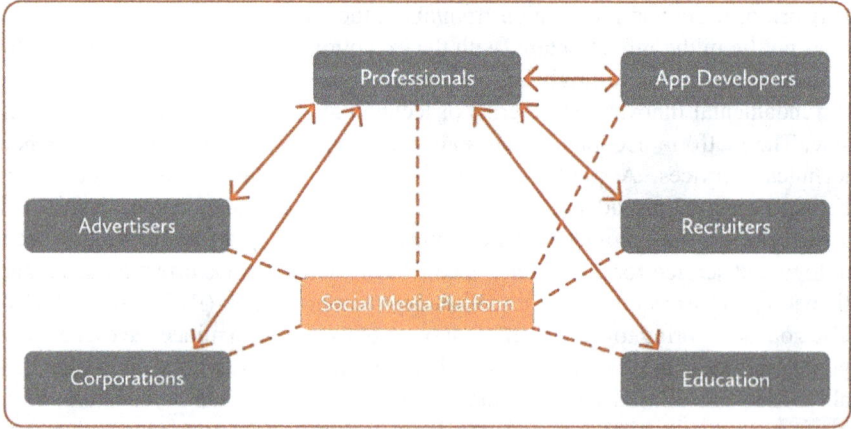

Fig. 5.1 From simple to complex network structures in the platform economy. (Source: Lecture Innovation, TU Wien, 2017, Hannes Werthner, Graphics © vielseitig.co.at)

contract risk. And intermediaries can usually also achieve better contract conditions due to better market knowledge and higher turnover.

It should also be noted that a successfully completed transaction increases the probability of a repetition between the parties involved: under behavioral assumptions for the participants such as bounded rationality and a probable opportunistic behavior (perhaps the partner does not have purely honest intentions) as well as general information asymmetry, a transaction is always associated with uncertainty. A successful transaction "interlocks" the parties involved. Williamson (1985) calls this information impactedness. Intermediaries have an important function, and this also explains—in the case of many market participants—their important role. Thus, platforms reduce transaction costs[1] and increase market efficiency.

A good example from the tourism sector is Booking.com: The platform has significantly reduced the disadvantages of information asymmetry for guests. It makes it easier for them to find and compare offers, with better prices and uniform conditions across different providers. There is also support for problems at the hotel with a good electronic service. Booking has thus virtually "democratized" the access for guests and enables them to obtain more favorable conditions than before. For providers, on the other hand, the situation is more difficult as they have to pay fees to the platform and face direct comparison with the competition. However, due to Booking's strong market position and the high demand on the platform, they are almost forced to participate.

The network effects,[2] where the value of participation grows with the number of participants, with their dynamics of the winner-take-all phenomenon, have led to a small number of actors dominating the market. They are the highest-valued companies worldwide today (Table 5.1). The large platforms, which focus on the processing of the transaction and not on production, are thus almost independent of the respective industry sector. Concrete products play an almost negligible role; they are virtualized, as are companies, entire markets, and increasingly also our society. In addition, the "information-based" nature of their business allows for easy scalability with an increase in transactions and sales without significant additional costs.

Table 5.1 shows on the left the current valuations (end of December 2024) and the outstanding importance of platform companies. For comparison, the situation in 2011 is shown in the right column, to illustrate the massive increase in the importance of platform companies. This structural change occurred between 2014 and 2016 was publicly evident and leaves one puzzled as to why the situation was not reacted to earlier.[3] A special case is NVIDIA, which is not one of the "classical" Web platform companies discussed so far. NVIDIA is an American company known for its graphics processing units (GPUs), AI technologies, and high-performance

---

[1] These are costs incurred in the initiation and processing of business transactions, such as the costs of searching for information, negotiating, concluding, transporting, and monitoring the transaction.

[2] This is described by Metcalfe's Law: it states that the value of a network is proportional to the square of the number of its users.

[3] Although it was already pointed out in 2010: Berners-Lee, T.: Long Live the Web: A Call for Continued Open Standards and Neutrality. *Scientific American*, December 1, 2010.

Table 5.1 Market capitalization (stock market value) of the top ten publicly traded companies (Financial Times Global 500)

Dec. 2024, Mio. USD		March 2011, Mio. USD	
Apple	**3,785,000**	Exxon Mobil	417,166
Nvidia	*3,785,000*	PetroChina	326,199
Microsoft	**3,134,000**	**Apple**	**321,072**
Alphabet	**2,331,000**	ICBC	251,078
Amazon	**2,307,000**[a]	Petrobras	247,417
Meta	**1,478,000**	BHP Billiton	247,079
Tesla	1,296,000[b]	China Constr. Bank	232,608
Broadcom[c]	*1,087,000*	Royal Dutch Shell	226,128
TSMC[d]	*1,024,000*	Chevron Corporation	215,780
Berkshire Hathaway[e]	978,890	**Microsoft**	**213,336**

Source: https://en.wikipedia.org/wiki/List_of_public_corporations_by_market_capitalization
© Hannes Werthner
Bold, platform companies; italic, IT product/service providers
[a] https://en.wikipedia.org/wiki/List_of_public_corporations_by_market_capitalization#cite_note-yam-46
[b] https://en.wikipedia.org/wiki/List_of_public_corporations_by_market_capitalization#cite_note-yt2-50
[c] American provider of a wide range of semiconductor and infrastructure software products
[d] Taiwan Semiconductor Manufacturing Company Limited
[e] American investment firm with CEO Warren Buffett

computing solutions. It is the global market leader in the area of GPUs, which are essential for AI. It offers also software solutions alongside its hardware to support a wide range of applications, from gaming to AI, robotics, and autonomous vehicles. Note that the table also contains bad news for Europe: There are no European companies included in this ranking.

These companies are active in several markets, such as online search, e-commerce, or cloud solutions, each with market shares of 50–90%.[4] The traditional media are a special case, as they are also active in the information business. They are particularly affected. Online advertising (a traditional media business) accounts for around 50% of total advertising expenditure, and around half of this went to just two online companies in 2023: Google and Meta.[5]

Platforms are also characterized by so-called lock-in effects: There are high costs if you want to switch to another system. It is not enough if a new market participant offers better quality and/or a lower price. It is also about data portability or data interoperability. Consumers and companies may not be able to transfer their "reputation capital" (e.g., ratings, trust values). It is also convenient for customers to deal only with few platforms, as it is less work and reduces complexity. On the one hand,

---

[4] This can also lead to cross-subsidization, such as when Google uses its profits from the advertising business to co-finance other divisions.
[5] https://de.statista.com/statistik/daten/studie/1311613/umfrage/anteil-des-werbeumsatzes-nach-unternehmen-weltweit/.

this means barriers to market entry for new competitors and, on the other, a dependency for the participating companies. For example, 80% of European small-and-medium-sized enterprises (SMEs) that sell online rely on well-known search engines as a means of marketing.

These companies are very active in research, development, and innovation and value the know-how factor. This also leads to many acquisitions of companies, especially start-ups; however, the products acquired in this way are not always used, but it is often a matter of "controlling" future competition. With their focus on research and development, they also represent major competition for universities, especially when it comes to the needed resources and to employing scientists. This is currently particularly evident in the field of AI and is also a problem in Europe in particular.

Platform as the Dominant Organizational Form in the Digital Age?

Online platforms have impacts on virtually all areas of our societal and economic life, on competition in the economy, the organization of companies, labor relations, technological innovation, and the nature and content of social and political discourse. They thus represent a kind of new institutional form, with large-scale effects and an asymmetric power over users, companies, as well as private individuals (Codagnone, 2023). This goes beyond the mere "market power." In particular, they have led to a restructuring of the media sector and in this way have gained immense societal and political power. They have become institutional ecosystems. Specifically, three levels or views on platforms can be identified (Dolata & Schrape, 2023):

1. The platform-operating companies as the organizing and structuring center, with the goal of a profitable business
2. The associated platforms as extensive, highly technically mediated social interaction spaces, not only for economic but also for political and social activities
3. The institutionalized coordination, control, and exploitation mechanisms of the platform operators, which connect these two previous levels of platform architecture

Against this background, some like Gawer (2022) assume that platform companies and their platform-based ecosystems will become the "dominant organizational form in the digital age." They are—as already shown—the organizers and owners of the already-mentioned public goods and spaces. We as individuals and companies must participate. This power is, once again summarized, exercised through:

Data: The immense data stocks are probably the largest "asset" of the platform companies. With this, they have the knowledge about us and our behavior but also about the market and the competition, in some sense our society as a whole.

They can thus shape their strategies, actions, and offers accordingly. This is particularly evident in their dominant role in the developing AI landscape.

Infrastructure and services: These companies exercise a gatekeeper function through their infrastructure (cloud and cloud access) and services. They decide on access and define largely autonomously the rules. As an example, one can take Google Maps with its range of services (cartographic data, integration possibility of these data, and corresponding services): It is de facto the sole basis for a multitude of private and public geographic services. Other providers have major competitive disadvantages. Another example is online health services: In the summer of 2020, with the introduction of COVID-19 tracing apps, national governments were dependent on cooperation with Apple and Google and forced to follow their rules.

Structuring of public discourse: Platform companies are restructuring the public sphere as mediators between politics and the population. Facebook, YouTube, Twitter, and Instagram are the guardians of the new controversial public sphere that they—these companies—have created. The traditional mass media have lost their power in communication. The new companies have an extreme influence on the political debate and our democracy through this restructuring and the establishment of the rules of communication that apply there.

Platforms and AI

The current competitive "race" in the field of AI also shows the strength of these platform companies and the rather high concentration in this area. At the same time, however, some movement can be observed in the field. The so-called open-weight models are worth mentioning here: this refers to LLMs where the trained weights (parameters of the model) are made publicly available. They are easier accessible and customizable, i.e., for fine-tuning for specific use cases. But also this type of models are partly developed by the big companies, e.g., Llama by Meta. The big AI players are these platform companies and start-ups, often associated with them in various ways. The costs for training a very large AI system like ChatGPT and the associated requirements for computing power and necessary data volumes are concentrated in their hands.

In Fig. 5.2, I sketch the structure of the currently developing AI landscape. I follow a value chain perspective, as found in the EU AI Act, and the explanations of Cusumano (2023). A value chain is a series of consecutive steps that lead to the production of a final product, from the initial design to delivery to the end customer. This chain is not necessarily linear but usually has a network structure.

Currently, the following main market (types of) participants can be identified. On the right in the figure, I include the two major customer segments, private individuals and companies or organizations such as administration and public institutions, without going into detail about them and the relationships between these segments:

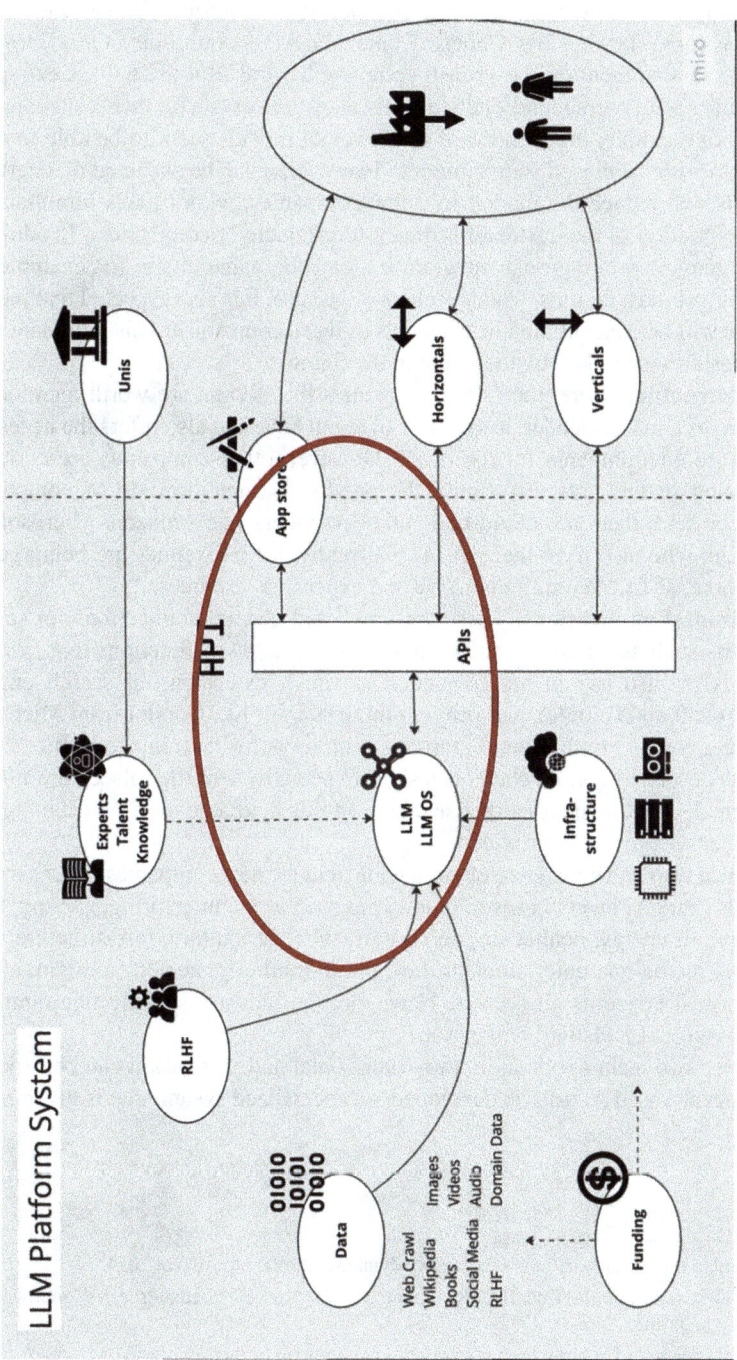

Fig. 5.2 The evolving AI landscape. (Own illustration together with Bernhard Krüpl-Sypien. © Hannes Werthner, Bernhard Krüpl-Sypien)

- **Foundation models/LLMs**: These companies provide the "basic technology" with the corresponding application interfaces (APIs). The main companies are currently OpenAI with Microsoft, Google, Meta, Amazon, Alibaba, Baidu, as well as some start-ups like Cohere, Contextual AI, or Anthropic.[6] On a European level, one can mention the French company Mistral. But the field is extremely dynamic, with permanently new models and services—with increased capabilities. For example, the mentioned open-weight models seem to be able to close the gap with the closed source model.[7] However, it can be expected that network effects will reduce the market to a few companies, with a likely simultaneous differentiation of the customer segment (consumers or companies). In addition, there may also be vertical integration along the value chain, for example, by offering cloud solutions, which is already the case. It is also expected that the app stores will be concentrated in the hands of these companies. This dominant market position is marked by the circle in the figure.
- **Infrastructure**: Here, the GPU[8] companies like Nvidia are worth mentioning, which, as a market leader, has a share of about 80% and also offers the necessary software environments for hardware. However, other companies are currently investing in this area, especially the previously mentioned LLM companies. Furthermore, there are cloud computing providers like Amazon, Microsoft, or Google, who also have their LLMs. Currently, large revenues are being generated here, as LLMs require massive and expensive resources.
- **Horizontal applications**: These are broad and general applications for several sectors, such as for access and combination with "own" functions (e.g., writing reports or also use in recommender systems), extensions of search engines (Microsoft and Google), and programming support like Copilot from Microsoft. There are also a multitude of start-ups with tools for text, image, audio, video, and code generation or chatbot design. Especially here, the places are not yet assigned, as in the next market segment. In this field, one may expect a big role for open-weight LLM providers.
- **Vertical applications**: Here opens a wide field for new companies or for services for old market players in several industries such as manufacturing, gaming, fashion, retail, energy, healthcare, defense, finance, agriculture, infrastructure, education, media and entertainment, law, programming, transport, tourism, etc. In essence, it concerns all sectors. Here, too, the industry-specific fine-tuning of open-weight LLMs will play a role.
- In these two main application areas (horizontal and vertical), it can be expected that agent-based AI will be developed—a specialized system that is given a spe-

---

[6] In particular, the list of start-ups is extremely dynamic. It refers to August 2024.
[7] https://www.reddit.com/r/LocalLLaMA/comments/1ebrdwa/closedsource_vs_openweight_models_by_maxime.
[8] Graphical Processor Unit: the hardware or chip requirement of this data-based AI.

cific task and can then complete it completely on its own. An example would be an agent that takes over travel planning based on user interests.[9]

- **Knowledge providers, especially universities**: These will probably need to cooperate with each other (see the Empire AI Consortium in the USA) as well as with the large companies; at the same, they will also be in direct competition with each other. This will affect both research and teaching. The exact role is not yet specified and will require a lot of (strategic) work, especially in countries that are not leaders in AI research (and most of them are). It may also happen, as is beginning to emerge, that universities will withdraw from this resource-intensive research and development.
- **Content providers**: This is a difficult and also legally contested field. There are of course the social media platforms and especially the large platforms with "their" data. However, these are again almost all positioned in the AI-LLM center. Currently, many Web data were "simply" used, and it is open how the ongoing legal copyright disputes will end. In addition, and specifically, the "public" data from public libraries and classical media are to be mentioned. These organizations are currently being overrun by the AI tsunami and feel helpless. With appropriate strategic reflection, however, they could realize that they and their high-quality data may be of central value. Whether they make something out of it is up to them.
- **RLHF (Reinforcement Learning From Human Feedback)**: It is expected that the current post-colonial division of labor with cheap training by people in the Global South will probably change—also due to public pressure.

The final business model or monetization seems still open. At the moment, the many investments are probably also due to competitive reactions according to a "Competitive Response" strategy, as defined by (Porter, 1980). Companies participate because others do and they don't want to miss anything. In addition, as I have already mentioned, there are also critical voices regarding the predicted growth rates and productivity increases through AI. In principle, revenue opportunities are opened up through the sale of horizontal and vertical applications, the sale of access to the models, the monetization of the knowledge gained through use, or the sale of model services to third-party providers. A lot is still in flux here.

Further risks for the individual market participants arise from direct competition with each other, open-source models, and also the development of geographically local models, for example, through the reaction of national states and corresponding subsidies—this is to be expected as a probable European response. Another risk may be the current regulatory activities at national and global level, especially how companies will deal with them.

Looking at this AI landscape, it is likely that a concentration will take place, in addition to cost and resource reasons. It also has convenience advantages for

---

[9] Interestingly, also this idea is already old, from the 1990s, with FIPA-ACL (Foundation for Intelligent Physical Agents-Agent Communication Language)—https://en.wikipedia.org/wiki/Agent_Communications_Language.

third-party providers and service developers in the respective network if they can concentrate on a few systems only. It is also likely that there will be no major qualitative restructuring at the level of the corporate landscape. There might be newcomers, but as it looks now, by and large, the players will remain the same. The currently dominant platform actors are active in several roles and have strengthened their respective positions.

It seems that for the first time in history since the industrial revolution, the corporate landscape may not be qualitatively restructured when the technology changes significantly, as it is now with AI. Compare this with the change in the early days, where IT has moved from the old mainframes to the PC or mobile phone. Most of the companies active at that time[10] no longer exist today, with the exception of IBM, albeit in a reduced and changed role. A comparison with other sectors such as the automotive industry is also interesting. There, too, a technological change toward IT-based e-mobility is taking place but with a change in the global corporate landscape, which is currently particularly negatively affecting the European automotive industry. Obviously, they missed the development toward software.

---

[10] Who still remembers UNIVAC or DEC (Digital Equipment Corporation) or Compaq?

Chapter 6
The System Is Failing

As we have seen, IT systems are extremely useful and successful. This was particularly evident during the COVID-19 pandemic—the world would probably have come to a standstill without IT tools: no work, no school, and no personal and public communication. In research, data science methods were indispensable for the development of effective vaccines. IT kept and keeps the system running, and it also serves to solve fundamental and vital problems. Just consider the essential role of informatics in achieving the United Nations' Sustainable Development Goals (SDGs).[1] Another example, also the subject of this book, is ChatGPT as an intelligent writing assistant that frees people from tedious writing and formulation tasks or the Web, which offers us almost "infinite" and free information, representing a public space that is also important for participation and the organization of civil society (described in Chap. 4). We see that this importance of IT is evident on an economic, political, and social level. At the same time, however, this development also has its downsides, as Tim Berners-Lee already noted in 2018 with his statement: "The System is Failing."[2] The list of critical and mutually dependent problems is long and not complete (Werthner et al., 2023). This applies both to digitalization in general and to AI in particular and can be taken as additional empirical evidence that AI is "just" another step in this complex socioeconomic-technical process of digital transformation:

- *Concentration on the Internet/Web*, where the already-described IT companies have a power that national governments can hardly control. These companies offer services that states cannot provide in this quality; they—and not the governments—decide on the implementation of essential services for the citizens, e.g., access to the mobile Web or to cloud services. They are representatives, as I have explained, of the platform economy, with its network effects and the

---

[1] sdgs.un.org/goals.
[2] *The Guardian*, March 12, 2018.

increase in market efficiency by reducing transaction costs. The production or the concrete product plays almost no role. It is also virtualized. Thus, informatics not only virtualizes products and companies but also entire markets and societies.

- The centralization of power on the net raises the question of personal, national, as well as geopolitical *sovereignty* (Werthner, 2022b; Timmers, 2024). These large companies decide on the implementation of important services. A very special and also enlightening example is the case of the Corona app in European countries, where Apple and Google, as the providers of mobile app stores, have decided on the architecture and functionality of these apps, and not these countries.[3] And their position as well as their influence may even become more powerful.

- *AI and automated decision-making*—simply put, the representation and automation of human thinking—lead to autonomous decision-making systems that raise significant legal and ethical questions (Larus et al., 2018). To complicate matters, in cases where AI is based on black box algorithms, we do not understand the result, i.e., the proposed and taken decisions.

- Autonomous, AI-based machines are entering warfare, leading to *autonomous weapons*. This can be clearly seen in the current technological developments in the wars in Ukraine and the Middle East. A worldwide ban, similar to that for chemical weapons, is already being discussed and seems necessary. Thus, the Secretary-General of the United Nations, António Guterres, has stated that "autonomous machines with the power to … take lives without human involvement … should be prohibited by international law."[4] It is worth mentioning that the civil and academic society has already reacted with the "Stop Killer Robots" campaign, initiated by AI researcher Toby Walsh.[5] Furthermore, one can observe how the Web itself is now increasingly being used as a weapon, as Berners-Lee again states: "The fact that power is concentrated among so few companies has made it possible to weaponise the web at scale."[6]

- This development toward the automation of thought and simultaneously the characteristic of IT, with these software components as part of the technology stack being able to control all machines, will have massive impacts on *employment relationships and jobs*, both qualitatively and quantitatively (Samaan, 2024). What are and will these new jobs be like? Will these tools enhance or replace our capabilities? We will have to regulate the distribution issues associated with this development and develop a new understanding of work and time. Moreover, the IT industry reproduces the colonial division of labor described by Tubaro et al. (2020), in which a large part of the low-skilled work is done outside

---

[3] Digital Humanism Online Lecture "Corona Contact Tracing—the Role of Governments and Tech Giants"; dighum.org/program-overview.

[4] António Guterres on Twitter, March 25, 2019; 6:28 PM.

[5] www.stopkillerrobots.org.

[6] Berners-Lee, T.: The Web is under threat. Join us and fight for it. In: World Wide Web Foundation, March 12, 2018; https://webfoundation.org/2018/03/web-birthday-29.

the rich metropolises (see also Munn, 2024).[7] Or consider the digital piecework or crowd work, where services are compensated in cent amounts via platforms, as well as the so-called gig economy with the mostly false self-assessment of independence and freedom of work, which in reality is often self-exploitation.

- The increasing *surveillance*, where we can observe massive violations of privacy, both by private companies and by state entities, is well described by Zuboff (2019) and Lindorfer (2024). It poses a great threat to democracy. But who can we trust, the big IT companies or the governments? Here, civil society and democratic institutions will play a key role. This shows that this development will require both legal and technical control measures. At the same time, the World Wide Web facilitates terrorist attacks, as it is already a means of military warfare. The topics of cybersecurity and data protection will permanently accompany us.
- In our online media, we observe developments such as the deliberate fabrication of *fake news* and the creation of *echo chambers* (Prem & Krenn, 2024). Originally intended for democratic and open communication and information exchange, these systems increasingly unfold and show their negative potential for political discourse and thus become a danger to democracy. This development is also a result of algorithms from the field of recommender systems, and the Web also reflects the prejudices of users in data and algorithms. While technical improvements (e.g., regarding fairness) appear possible, especially with the algorithms, dealing with fake news and the use of the Web for unfair political influence will lead to massive political disputes, especially with a focus on future political online decision-making processes. Here, one finds the ever-present tension between content moderation (when does this become censorship) and free expression of opinion.[8]
- These developments in IT represent a *significant environmental burden*. Although there are already a number of positive examples of IT being used for climate protection measures (reducing energy consumption through better machine controls, long-range data collection and simulation models, etc.) and improving the efficiency of power consumption in data centers, the negative environmental impacts of IT should currently be of great concern—such as the effects of blockchain technology, for which coal-fired power plants that had already been shut down have been reactivated. In AI, training with large datasets and "daily" use cause a lot of energy consumption; for example, a ChatGPT request ("prompt") requires between 50 and 90 times more energy than a normal Web search.[9] This

---

[7] Cassili, A.: Digital Humanism Lecture—What is a 'Truly Ethical' Artificial Intelligence? An end-to-end approach to responsible and humane technological systems, 2021; dighum.org/program-overview.

[8] See also the discussion on Section 230 of the CDA (Communications Decency Act). This established in 1996 that operators of Internet platforms cannot be held liable for the content of their users. The aim was to prevent restrictions on freedom of speech, as defined in the first amendment to the US Constitution, with all the now questionable results.

[9] https://limited.systems/articles/google-search-vs-chatgpt-emissions/, according to: Der Standard, September 27, 2024.

then leads to the fact that in Ireland, for example, the data centers located there will consume 21% of the country's total electricity in 2023.[10]

This list could be continued with more points. They are all interrelated and must be addressed together in order to exploit the positive potential of digitalization. This does not happen by itself—it is up to us, as individuals and as a society, to decide which direction we go.

---

[10] *The Guardian*, July 23, 2024.

Chapter 7
Digital Humanism and the Vienna Manifesto

These "two faces" of IT, their undeniable enormous achievements as well as future potentials and at the same time their obvious misdevelopments, were the motivation for the first Vienna Workshop on Digital Humanism in April 2019 (Werthner, 2022a). The intellectual starting point was our responsibility as scientists (Popper, 1969), which calls on us to shape technologies according to human values and needs, instead of allowing technologies to shape humans. The workshop was also inspired by the tradition of the Vienna Circle, a multidisciplinary approach in early-twentieth-century Vienna that reflected on the revolutionary impact of science on our understanding of the world and thus had a major influence on the further development of science (Sigmund, 2017).

More than 100 participants from the academic-scientific field, from public institutions, civil society, and industry, participated in the two-day workshop. The program dealt with the history and impact of IT and informatics, as well as their dynamics and future. The discussions focused on technical, political, economic, social, ethical, and legal issues. A real gain was the presence of a wide variety of disciplines, including political science, law, sociology, history, anthropology, philosophy, management science, and informatics. At the center of the discussion was the relationship between computer science and society or, as it was called during the workshop, the coevolution of IT and human. The discussion showed that computer science is important, but not sufficient to provide comprehensive answers; rather, a broad, interdisciplinary approach is required. The participants were also convinced that it is possible to influence these developments; indeed, that it is our responsibility to do so.

The term *digital humanism* was deliberately chosen to refer to the concepts of humanism and the Enlightenment, according to which people are responsible for their actions and beliefs and are the focus of attention (Nida-Rümelin & Weidenfeld, 2018; Nida-Rümelin & Winter, 2024; Nida-Rümelin & Staudacher, 2024; Prem, 2024). We emphasize the importance of rational and critical thinking, also a reference to the Vienna Circle and its logical empiricism. We humans have the freedom, the right, and therefore also the responsibility to make use of our own power of thought and to act accordingly.[1] We are the authors of our own lives. Personal autonomy and decision-making freedom are the prerequisites for an open, democratic, and ecologically sustainable society. The technological progress is neither God-given nor does it follow a technical or economic determinism. We as individuals and as a society should and must make decisions taking into account democratic, humanistic, and ecological considerations. It is our task to shape technologies in line with our human values and needs, rather than allowing technologies to shape us humans. We define *digital humanism as an approach that describes, analyzes, and, most importantly, influences the complex interplay of technology and humankind, for a better sustainable society and life, fully respecting universal human right.*

Digital humanism is intended to inspire the developments of our society, which is largely dependent on digital technologies (Werthner et al., 2022a, b). In this sense, we distinguish digital humanism from digital humanities, the study of human society and culture in the humanities using digital means, i.e., the use of digital tools in the humanities and social sciences. In contrast, digital humanism aims to rethink our current digital practices, including research, development, and innovation in the digital field. As such, it pursues the positivist goal that technology creates societal progress and not just innovation for the sake of growth.

From a historical perspective, the term *humanism* refers to two different movements. The first denotes the time between the middle of the fifteenth and the end of the sixteenth century, the epoch of Renaissance Humanism, in which antiquity was rediscovered in the arts, and in philosophy and scholars, philosophers and artists referred to themselves as "humanists." Aesthetics and ethics now focused on man and no longer on the supernatural or divine. The most famous iconic representation of humanism is the *Vitruvian Man* by Leonardo da Vinci (see Fig. 7.1), in which a man in a circle is depicted as the archetype for the principles of harmony and proportion represented in Vitruvius' book *De architectura*.

A second period of humanism flourished in the era of the Enlightenment, at the end of the eighteenth century. The French Revolution was largely inspired by the principles of human freedom and democracy, which were rooted in the humanistic spirit of that time. Humanism was associated with educational and pedagogical ideals that focused on values such as human dignity and humanity. The two movements of course have a number of common concepts and interests, which are still relevant for digital humanism today, such as a strong focus on human rights and their preservation in the digital field.

However, there are also critics of these classical notions of humanism. Above all, the educational ideal of the humanists is questioned, as it supports the belief in the cultural supremacy of Europe and the "West." In addition, the focus on the human subject always requires a critical examination of the question of who exactly this subject is and which of its many properties should be considered essential. Moreover,

---

[1] Freedom, responsibility, and reason are interconnected: Because we are rational, i.e., we have the ability for reason-guided thinking and action, we are free through this ability, and because we are free, we also have responsibility.

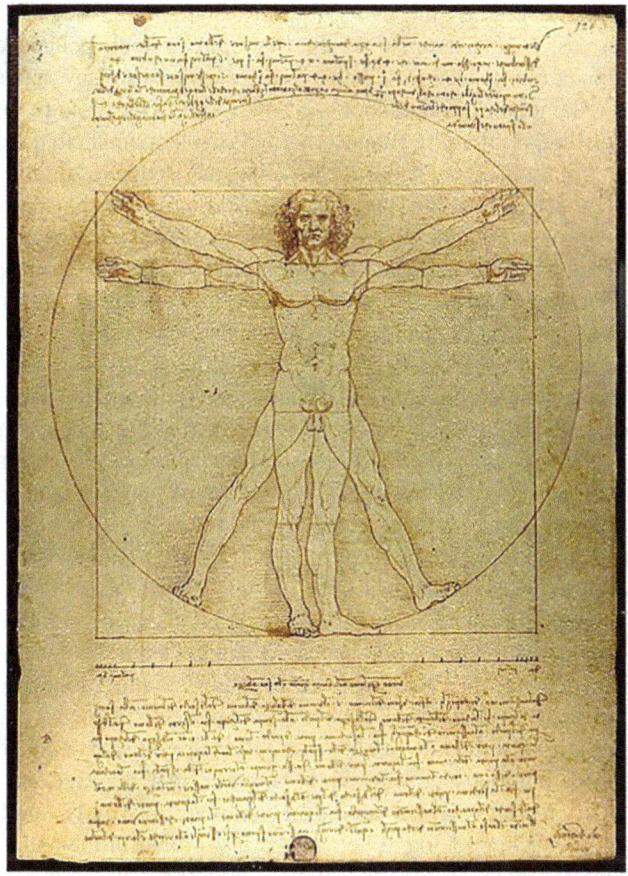

Fig. 7.1 Vitruvian Man after Leonardo da Vinci. (Source: https://de.wikipedia.org/wiki/Vitruvianischer_Mensch#/media/Datei:Da_Vinci_Vitruve_Luc_Viatour.jpg © public domain)

in times of ecological crisis, the focus on man, who is the cause of this crisis, can rightly be objected to. But today's digital humanism does not see a "dominance" of man over nature or a colonial mission; on the contrary, it is critical of existing colonial tendencies in today's digital technologies and their current negative impacts on the environment. This is evident, for example, in our attitude toward digital sovereignty and geopolitics. The question of which human traits should be focused on is also a subject of discussion in digital humanism, especially since the relationship between individual, society, and nature is one of its main concerns.

Digital humanism must also be aware of the Critical Theory of the Frankfurt School in the context of the Enlightenment. Its prominent representatives Theodor W. Adorno and Max Horkheimer provided a critical analysis of the process of empowerment through rationality, and the resulting demystification would in principle apply to any technological process aimed at increasing the power of the individual. This is certainly the case with most digital technologies. But already Jürgen Habermas, a later member of the Frankfurt School, pointed out that the demystification of rationalism would also mean rejecting its many important contributions to law, democracy, and science—and thus also to technology. One can even draw an interesting, reinforcing connection of digital humanism to the dialectics of Enlightenment: individual decisions are an important source of digital innovation, but this source can also lead to a dangerous increase in power to manipulate masses collectively. Moreover, digital humanists also warn of the power of the caste of the knowing (according to Horkheimer and Adorno) or, as they might also put it today, of the power of the platforms. It is precisely here that digital humanism argues for broad democratic participation and involvement. And where abstraction as a tool for manipulation and formulas as tools for creating predictability were identified, digital humanism now has similar concerns about digital tools and big data abstractions (see Peterson et al., 2023; Chap. 3). Machine abstraction has become a prerequisite for dealing with the complexity of our world. The adaptation of such abstractions in IT to human values and to the complexity of our natural environment is a core goal of digital humanism, and it remains a task for the future.

Digital humanism rejects both the mechanistic and the animistic paradigm—man is not a machine, and machines are not humans (Nida-Rümelin & Staudacher, 2024). The human as machine is an old metaphor. It dates back to the early modern period. Mechanism makes the world appear as a large deterministic clockwork and man as a cog in this machine. Nothing is left to chance. In this view, there is no room for human freedom, responsibility, and reason. Applied to humans, the normative foundations of morality and law would prove to be pure illusion or collective human self-deception. In a humanistic worldview, however, man is a free and responsible agent in interaction with other humans and a common social and natural world. The other view—the machine is like a human—is also found in the anthropomorphic view of AI, the machine "learns" or "knows"; both can only be done by humans. This "humanization" is already criticized early in the 1960s by Weizenbaum with his program ELIZA (see Chap. 2). In the animistic paradigm, the AI system is endowed with mental properties, as long as its external (output) behavior is sufficiently similar to that of humans; this is currently the case in data-based AI.

Digital humanism is still young and has different historical roots. But it is a fundamental concept that is about our future as people and as a society, not only in the digital world. It is therefore not just an academic task but a societal and political concern. It is not just about science, research, and innovation. Equally important are education, communication, and influencing the public to promote democratic participation. This means that digital humanism is relevant to a diverse audience, from scientists and policy makers to industry, institutions, civil society, and non-governmental organizations.

These ideas are very well reflected in the *Vienna Manifesto for Digital Humanism* (see also Appendix).[2] It is the result of the Vienna Workshop, has been signed by

---

[2] dighum.org/dighum-manifesto.

people from over 50 countries, and is now available in 10 languages. The manifesto is also a call for collective action to mobilize support across national borders and continents to create a more humane and sustainable future. The principles of the Vienna Manifesto include:

Data Protection, Democracy, and Inclusion

- Digital technologies should be designed and used to promote democracy, inclusion, and participation.
- Privacy and freedom of speech are fundamental values that should be at the center of our actions.

Regulation and Public Control

- Regulatory authorities must intervene to break up technology monopolies.
- Decisions whose consequences affect individual or that could affect collective human rights must continue to be made by people.

Role of Science and Research

- It is necessary to integrate various disciplines and eliminate discipline-specific silos in order to master our current societal, economic, and environmental challenges.
- Universities are the places where new knowledge is created and critical thinking is practiced. They should break down the boundaries between the disciplines and promote their collaboration with a view to a holistic view of technological development.

Education

- We need new curricula that connect humanities and social sciences with technical and engineering subjects.
- Education in the IT field and dealing with the ethical and societal impacts of IT must begin as early as possible.

As you can see, digital humanism is trying not only to eliminate the dark sides of this IT-induced change but also to promote innovation focused on people and society as well as nature, for a more livable world and for a better and sustainable society.

Chapter 8
The Digital Humanism Initiative

Our workshop and the manifesto have obviously touched on a hot topic. The national and international response was enormous and diverse. Not only academics from the field of computer science, but also from many other disciplines responded; civil society, funding bodies, institutions and political decision-makers have also expressed their interest. At the same time, we began to network and cooperate with a number of international initiatives with similar goals, e.g., HAI (Human-Centered Artificial Intelligence) in Stanford,[1] Dutch Digital Society,[2] Web Science Trust,[3] People-Centered Internet,[4] and Digital Enlightenment Forum.[5] With the latter three, we formed a "formal alliance," Humanity Internet Alliance (HIA), for joint activities.

In particular, the topic of AI, and with it also digital humanism, is now "mainstream" in politics, with international discussions and activities on the risks of the development, possible rules up to regulations as well as research and innovation programs, and impacts on geopolitics. The growing public awareness is also reflected in several international political actions, e.g., in the USA with some antitrust lawsuits and in Europe with EU regulations such as *Digital Service Act*, *Digital Markets Act*, *EU AI Act*, or the European *General Data Protection Regulation*. These legislative initiatives try to define rules in the largely unregulated online world and to implement them (see Chap. 9). Further examples in this direction are the *OECD Principles on AI*, activities of UNESCO, the UN's view of the Internet as a global public good, or the global initiative *Partnership on AI*.[6] International

---

[1] hai.stanford.edu.
[2] www.thedigitalsociety.info.
[3] webscience.org.
[4] peoplecentered.net.
[5] digitalenlightenment.org.
[6] A discussion and description of all these initiatives go far beyond this book, as the list is certainly not complete and would need to be constantly updated.

© The Author(s), under exclusive license to Springer Nature Switzerland AG 2025
H. Werthner, *Digital Humanism*, https://doi.org/10.1007/978-3-031-86905-1_8

standardization organizations also became active, e.g., IEEE with its *IEEE 7000 Software Engineering Standard*.[7]

Concrete reactions—and they reflected that the initiative started in Austria—came from Austrian and regional government agencies and institutions: The Vienna government included digital humanism in its future strategy, and the Vienna Science and Technology Fund (WWTF), a partner from the very beginning, operates a research program and also finances a doctoral college on digital humanism. The Austrian federal government signed the *Poysdorf Declaration* on Digital Humanism, a joint declaration of the foreign ministers of Austria, the Czech Republic, and Slovakia. The importance of the topic is also shown by the fact that there are already dedicated research positions and professorships at universities and universities of applied sciences: A UNESCO Chair for Digital Humanism was established at TU Vienna; furthermore, there is a scholarship program of the IWM (Institute for Human Sciences) funded by the Ministry of Climate. The topic also found its reflection in the Austrian corporate landscape, with the CEO dialogue, with practical implementation initiatives around https://www.msg-plaut.com/at/digitaler-humanismus, the publication "The Practice of Digital Humanism" (Krause, 2023), and a Digital Humanism Practice Award.

During the pandemic, our activities went online. Since 2020, we organized over 60 *DigHum Online Lectures* (150 h available online). This lecture series became a real success and has significantly contributed to the international discussion, with a large number of participants and internationally renowned speakers. There was a broad range of topics from AI and ethics, limits of AI, COVID-19 apps and privacy, efficiency and resilience to AI regulation in Europe, automation and work, or autonomous weapons to the question of sovereignty in the digital world (sdgs.un.org/goals).[127] In addition, we organized *conferences* such as "Can Machines Save the World?" (November 2023), "Digital Humanism Summit on AI and Democratic Sustainability" (July 2023), or the "Paradigm Shift in Computer Science (Nov 2024).[8]

Furthermore, we have published the two *anthologies* "Perspectives on Digital Humanism" (Werthner et al. 2022b) and "Introduction to Digital Humanism" (Werthner et al., 2024) as open-access publications with currently already over 1,170,000 downloads,[9] created a "Roadmap for Digital Humanism—Research, Innovation and Teaching" (Prem et al., 2022), and organized several successful international *Summer Schools*. Finally, we published a German textbook for high school and adult education (Eichinger et al., 2024). This is now translated into several languages.

The most important result, however, is that we have succeeded in creating an international intellectual core of digital humanism, which consists of the authors of the manifesto, the members of our international program committee, organizational

---

[7] Here, the Austrian informatics professor Sarah Spiekermann is the leading person.

[8] All the material is available at dighum.ec.tuwien.ac.at/lectures-program and www.youtube.com/channel/UC-oCPW9l7IuDvu_J30tqMVw.

[9] As of the end of January 2025.

partners, the authors of our various publications, and the speakers as well as the participants of our online lecture series on digital humanism. This truly vibrant group is growing and is active; see also our statement on ChatGPT from March 2023[10] or in support of the EU AI Act from December 2023.[11] This international group is the Digital Humanism Initiative.

Short History of Digital Humanism

In the short history of the idea and concept of digital humanism, a development path from a philosophical and cultural-historical view to the broader interdisciplinary-technical view as defined in the Viennese Manifesto can be recognized. Thus, the first important contributions came from Milad Doueihi, a church historian and holder of the chair for research on digital cultures at the University of Paris-Sorbonne. He dealt with the question of how culture is changed by digital technologies and emphasized the convergence of cultural heritage and digital technology (Doueihi, 2011); thus, the focus was more on an expanded version of the digital humanities. A completely different development strand is represented by the consulting firm Gartner, which used the term "Digital Humanism" for its focus on customers and customer integration (Customer Experience) in 2015. In Austria, however, as early as 2017, Christoph Thun-Hohenstein, cultural manager and Austrian top official, advocated for human-oriented innovation and change using the term.[12]

A significant contribution was made by the philosopher Julian Nida-Rümelin and the cultural and communication scientist Nathalie Weidenfeld in 2018 with their book *Digital Humanism*, based on a philosophical and media-scientific perspective, with a critical discussion of AI and the clear separation of human and machine. The topic was also picked up by the Austrian technology—and art festival Ars Electronica in Linz in 2019, here in the art—and cultural-scientific context. In Vienna, a study by the WWTF commissioned by the city of Vienna (Strassnig et al., 2019) was published in July 2019, which aimed to identify topics and actors of digital humanism.

The central event for the further development was then the workshop on digital humanism in April 2019 at the TU Wien, where the different perspectives were also taken up and which ended with the adoption of the Viennese Manifesto. Initiated also by discussions with the high-profile international Advisory Board of the Faculty of Informatics at TU Wien, the workshop provided a broad and also

---

[10] ChatGPT—a catalyst for what kind of future? caiml.org/dighum/statement-of-the-digital-humanism-initiative-on-chatgpt.

[11] Public DigHum Statement on the EU AI Act; caiml.org/dighum/statement-on-ai-act/.

[12] https://www.creativeaustria.at/2017/01/01/ideas-for-change/.

operationalizable definition of the term, which allows a comprehensive view of digital humanism. It was also the starting point of the Digital Humanism Initiative. This history also shows how digital humanism has developed from an idea to an influential international movement.

Chapter 9
It's Simple, It's Complicated

The aim of digital humanism is to eliminate the downsides of digitalization as far as possible and at the same time to use this technological development for a fairer society and a better life. This objective is straightforward and sounds simple, but implementing it and putting the development on the right track is complicated and challenging. This includes (1) legal and regulatory frameworks and objectives for the organization of the development on a technical, economic, and political level and (2) technical-constructive tasks for the design and implementation of technology. Both aspects complement and depend on each other; this is part of the complexity of shaping the digital future. In the following, I therefore consider these two essential fields of action and the challenges associated with them.

Regulatory Frameworks and Legal Approaches

There exist already a multitude of guidelines, principles, and regulations. In addition to international frameworks, over 50 states have already formulated national guidelines of "some" kind (at least). Examples include the USA, where several agencies have intensified their efforts to regulate AI, or also Saudi Arabia and Argentina, which have published draft regulations on deepfakes and the responsible use of AI. Politics, after decades of "non-regulation" of the digital world, has reacted surprisingly quickly to the technical and market development of AI. It almost seems like a startled awakening.

In the question of regulating platforms and cyberspace in general, not just AI, the EU plays a pioneering role. In part, its guidelines and laws serve as templates in other regions, so one also speaks of a Brussels effect here (Bradford, 2019). Therefore, I start with the EU's activities for "rule-setting" for large platform companies and their regulation of AI, followed by an overview of international initiatives for AI guidelines. This chapter is intended as an overview. Further information can be found in Rotenberg (2024) and Müller and Kettemann (2024). My comments are also based on these publications.[1]

Regulation of Platforms I: Digital Services Act (DSA)

After the European Union had taken a rather liberal stance on digital markets for years, it has significantly changed this position, especially toward platforms and also in recognition of their economic power. The DSA, together with the DMA (Digital Markets Act), is an expression of this strategy for a safer digital space in which the fundamental rights of all users and citizens are protected and equal starting conditions for all participants are given. The DSA specifically aims to limit the "social" discursive power of the platforms and became legally effective in November 2022. A significant innovation is the "extraterritorial" scope of the DSA, which is tied to the location of the user and not to the location of the respective service provider. Therefore, it is now possible to conduct legal disputes in Europe and not in the country where the provider has its company record. The DSA identifies digital platforms as responsible actors in the fight against illegal online content and thus assigns them a special role.[2] It lays down rules for transparency, accountability, and due diligence, such as specific requirements for terms and conditions, the establishment of a compliance management system, or reporting and transparency requirements. These obligations depend on the size of the platforms and their role in the online world, with the full range of obligations applying to very large online platforms and very large online search engines with more than 45 million users. The law also introduces a number of rules for implementation, an obligation to cooperate with the Commission, and possible sanctions and other enforcement options. This is an important innovation, as are the far-reaching powers granted to the European Commission to enforce the rules for very large online platforms and search engines. This includes the ability to conduct investigations and inspections or to impose high fines. It is therefore not a toothless instrument.

Regulation of Platforms II: Digital Markets Act (DMA)

The DMA was enacted at the same time as the DSA, both belonging together. The DMA tries to curb the economic power of the Big Tech platforms. A significant innovation is that the DMA moves from the so-called ex post approach (i.e., the authorities must first identify a violation and then react) to an ex ante approach and accordingly prohibits or orders regulations for a lot of practices considered

---

[1] For a current overview of international news on AI, I recommend the newsletter of the "Center for AI and Digital Policy" (https://www.caidp.org/).

[2] The DSA is based on the EU E-Commerce Directive and extends it.

"harmful." These obligations do not apply to all platforms but only to the so-called gatekeepers. These are characterized by the following features: (1) they have significant influence, (2) they offer a so-called core platform service,[3] and (3) they have a solid and permanent position. For all these properties, there are defined and specific thresholds. The obligations to be observed include, for example, the prohibition of merging data from different own services or forcing users to use a certain payment service. The European Commission as the supervisory authority can further define and specify additional obligations, such as enabling users to easily transfer their own data to another provider (data portability). The new regulations can also be enforced, with regular violations also resulting in fines, up to 10% of the worldwide annual turnover. In addition, the DMA prohibits mergers of companies and, as a last resort, may break up gatekeeper companies if the obligations of the DMA are systematically violated.

Regulation of AI: EU AI Act

The EU AI Act is—alongside AI regulation in China—the first comprehensive regulation on AI by a major regulatory authority worldwide. The regulation is innovative in that it follows a risk-based approach, with tiered regulations depending on the risk category. The law came into effect on August 1, 2024, after long and tough negotiations between the EU Commission, the European Parliament, and the member states. At the end of the negotiations, it was additionally blocked by Germany, France, and Italy to "protect" their AI companies.[4] But these issues could be resolved. The majority of the rules come into effect after 2 years, with rules concerning unacceptable risks already in February 2025.

Figure 9.1 shows the risk categories of the AI Act. In the first risk category, AI systems are classified as *unacceptable* if they influence the free will of users or include "social scoring," i.e., the AI-supported monitoring and evaluation of individual citizens' behavior by state authorities. According to the scope of the AI law that came into effect in August 2024, their use in the EU is then prohibited. For the next group, AI systems with *high risk*, the scope of use is of greater importance—i.e., not the AI system itself is considered risky but the area in which it is used. Examples include decisions about access to education or employment, law enforcement, or migration. If an AI system falls into this category, its manufacturers and professional users (those providing services to other parties) must comply with a number of obligations, such as setting up risk and quality management systems. Such a system must also be registered with the EU Commission.

In the third group, systems with *limited risk*, "only" transparency obligations are provided for. Providers must inform their users that the content was generated by an

---

[3] Such services are, for example, online search engines, online social networks, video-sharing platforms, or cloud services.

[4] 136 Quite a few suspect the lobbying influence of the large platform companies behind this.

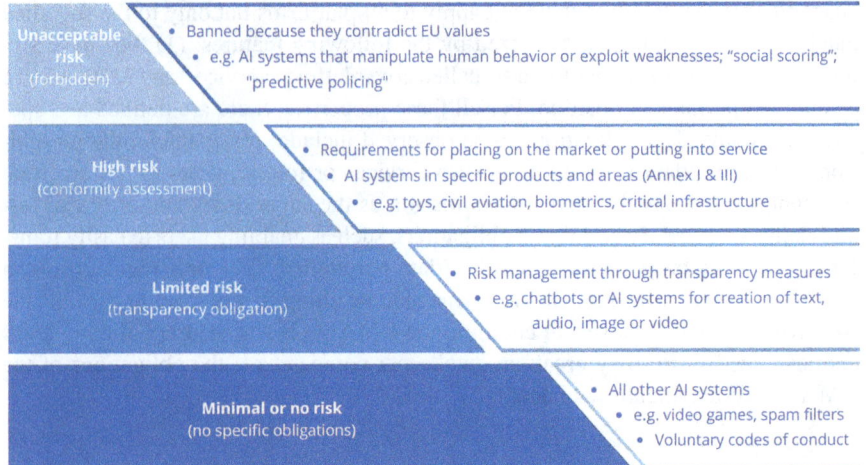

Fig. 9.1 EU AI Act: AI systems are categorized according to their risk potential as unacceptable, high, limited, and minimal/no risk. (Source: https://www.rtr.at/rtr/service/ki-servicestelle/ai-act/risikostufen_ki-systeme.de.html ©RTR, CC BY 4.0)

AI.[5] Finally, *risk-free AI systems* (group 4) are not regulated by the AI Act. These include, for example, spam filters for email programs. Here, the risk for users is considered to be so low that no regulations are envisaged.

However, the law does not cover all areas of AI application—military applications are generally excluded, which can be fatal given the increasing importance of AI in warfare. In addition, there are a number of other exceptions, such as the possibility of biometric remote identification in certain threat situations. These exceptions were also claimed by the member states in the final round of negotiations with the European parliament. Is the glass now half empty or half full? Rather the latter, it is an important step in the EU's overall system for regulating the digital space, giving politicians effective tools to enforce against the omnipotence of large platforms and NGOs the opportunity to observe and intervene. We will see how these are used.

AI Regulation in China[6]

In recent years, China has developed a comprehensive and detailed regulatory regime for AI. It is based on several guidelines and laws, written by ministries, specially created organizations, but also the Communist Party, and all of it with the

---

[5] Interestingly, the democracy-endangering deepfake detection falls also into this category.

[6] This only provides a brief overview; a more detailed discussion would go beyond the scope of this book. For those interested, check Zhang (2024).

participation of experts and scientists. This framework covers both ethical and practical aspects of technology development. It serves not only to control the technology and steer its development or address social and economic impacts but also to assume an international leadership role for China in the field of AI. It thus also has a competitive geopolitical background, as it also exists in the other regions and power centers of this world. However, the regulatory regime clearly stipulates that AI technologies must not violate state interests.

The Chinese government also aims to gain more control over the online world and curb the power of the—as in the "West" increasingly influential—private platform companies. Thus, anti-competitive practices and especially illegal publications of user data were stopped. However, it should be noted that privacy in China is not an individual right but is rather considered as a common, state good. This follows from Chinese tradition and also corresponds to the view of the Communist Party. However, complaints from citizens are also increasing in China, which seems to be increasingly aligning Chinese data protection with the European General Data Protection Regulation. Since March 2022, China also regulates recommendation algorithms that filter content, control search results, set prices, and recommend videos. In this context, I am not discussing the Chinese social credit system, which is actually an adaptation of credit security mechanisms from the USA, Japan, and Europe—see Warnke and Woesler (2024). Ultimately, however, it is an attempt at cybernetic economic and societal control. Interestingly, there were already such technological attempts in the field of economic planning in Allende's Chile in the early 1970s, which were prematurely thwarted by Pinochet's machine guns.

This brief overview shows that China, like the EU, is taking a structured and comprehensive approach to regulation of AI is pursued. At the same time, the Chinese position on regulation is criticized by the "Western" states, accusing it of lacking orientation toward values such as democratic participation.[7]

International Governance Proposals for AI

While Europe has a concrete, enforceable law with the EU AI Act, the "global" international discussion is moving within the framework of principles and recommendations, also because these international organizations do not have implemented enforcement possibilities.

Overall, the discussion has developed very rapidly, especially also under the influence of the launch of ChatGPT. Starting from the Ethics Guidelines for AI of the EU from 2018, the AI principles of the OECD/G20 from 2019, to the UNESCO recommendation on AI ethics from the year 2021, governments have agreed on the basic norms and principles for the regulation of AI and its services. Likewise, the

---

[7] It remains to be seen to what extent this is a rather ideological "geopolitical" criticism and to what extent there will be rapprochement at international level (e.g., through the UN).

scope of AI governance models has expanded over time. From the initial focus on "human-centered and trustworthy AI" to the recognition of "fairness, accuracy, and transparency" as building blocks for AI governance, we now see the consideration of sustainability, gender equality, and employment as further key categories. This number of guidelines and principles is relatively complex. They are proposed by different organizations with different legal frameworks and enforcement possibilities, and they overlap with known legal issues such as consumer protection, copyright, national security, and data protection. Aligning and adapting all of this, in addition to implementation and enforcement, presents a major challenge.

UNESCO Recommendations for AI

These recommendations by UNESCO are understood as the first globally negotiated international law text on the subject of AI ethics—this is the reason I will explain them in more detail. They were adopted in November 2021 by the member states and are considered a groundbreaking recommendation on the ethics of AI. The goal of AI systems should be to serve the common good, with an ethical compass and a comprehensive normative foundation for global rules.[8] The recommendations are the result of a multi-year process, also with the participation of many experts and NGOs. According to UNESCO, the digital transformation should promote human rights and contribute to the Sustainable Development Goals of the UN. They address issues of transparency, accountability, and data protection and link this with more action-oriented chapters on data governance, education, culture, work, health, and economy. And these recommendations also introduced new guarantees, such as for gender justice and sustainability. Key recommendations include:

- Data protection: Measures should be taken that go beyond the steps taken so far by technology companies and governments to guarantee individuals a greater protection and to ensure transparency, empowerment, and control over their own personal data.
- Prohibition of social scoring and mass surveillance: The explicit recommendation is thus the prohibition of this type of AI systems.
- Monitoring and evaluation: The recommendation provides for new tools, which should help in the implementation, including ethical impact assessments.
- Protection of the environment: AI actors should prefer data-, energy-, and resource-efficient AI methods. AI should be a more important tool in the fight against climate change and in addressing environmental problems.

The recommendations aim at the peaceful use of AI systems and establish four "values": (1) respect, protection, and promotion of human rights and fundamental freedoms as well as human dignity, (2) promotion of the environment and ecosystems,

---

[8] https://www.unesco.at/science/science-and-bioethics/ethics-of-artificial-intelligence/unesco-recommendation-on-the-ethics-of-ai.

(3) ensuring diversity and inclusion, as well as (4) living in a peaceful and just society. In addition, ten principles are mentioned: proportionality and harm avoidance, safety, fairness and non-discrimination, sustainability, right to privacy and data protection, human oversight and ultimate responsibility, transparency and explainability, responsibility and accountability, public awareness, and digital education. Red lines are also drawn for the use, such as the prohibition of social scoring or mass surveillance.

The recommendations thus define ethical values and principles. In terms of concrete implementation, UNESCO can only urge and encourage its member states to take appropriate actions, such as ensuring implementation; it cannot "force" them. This also applies to other organizations like the OECD/G20 with their AI principles.[9]

Council of Europe and UNO

The Council of Europe, founded in 1949, is an international organization for the protection of human rights, democracy, and the rule of law in Europe. It has drafted the European Convention on Human Rights, which states must recognize before they can become members of the Council of Europe, and it also hosts the European Court of Human Rights.[10] Currently, it has 46 member states, 27 of which are also in the EU. Together with countries like the USA or Japan and many experts and civil society organizations, it has now drafted an AI Convention. This is a legally binding treaty that the signatory states would have to adhere to.[11] The contracting parties commit themselves to respect the AI principles already known from UNESCO recommendations, such as the protection of human dignity and individual autonomy, transparency, accountability and responsibility, equality and non-discrimination, and the protection of privacy when developing and using AI systems. The initial signing took place on September 5, 2024, by countries such as the UK, the USA, Norway, and Israel, as well as the EU, and more countries will follow. This agreement—as ambitious as it sounds—is, however, significantly "weaker" than the EU AI Act, and according to expert opinion, the impact on US IT platforms may be minimal.[12]

The UNO plays a special role, as it includes all states of this world, especially China. As some attribute to AI similar potentials as nuclear energy, so from this perspective, a successful regulation can only be global. Therefore, the UN is indispensable in this context. The UN General Assembly adopted a global resolution on AI on March 21, 2024, with a large majority, in which member states are called upon to protect human rights and personal data and to monitor AI for possible damages. In addition, the UN Secretary-General has established a "High Level" AI advisory board, which delivered its final report "Governing AI for Humanity" in

---

[9] https://www.oecd-ilibrary.org/docserver/eb55842c-de.pdf.
[10] It has also developed an international cybercrime convention and a data protection convention.
[11] https://rm.coe.int/1680afae3c.
[12] Barry O'Sullivan, University College Cork, Ireland; www.newsweek.com/us-signs-international-ai-treaty-tech-industry-impact-1949951.

September 2024.[13] This report also contains many of the known principles, but it rightly emphasizes the need for a global approach. It envisages a global, inclusive AI governance framework based on international cooperation, with light institutional mechanisms to support ongoing efforts. The report also contains seven concrete "operational" recommendations for action, such as the establishment of a scientific body, similar to the International Panel on Climate Change (IPCC), to assess the impact of AI, an AI capacity network,[14] a global AI fund, an AI data framework, or a regular policy dialogue on AI governance. This report very well illustrates the globally growing recognition of the importance of AI and the need to steer this development and not leave everything up to the market. At the same time, however, it also highlights the "limitations" of the UN, which has very little directive power and depends on global cooperation.

Brief Summary of the Legal and Regulatory Frameworks

All these laws, guidelines, and recommendations on AI resemble each other in their focus but differ in their legal enforceability. Currently, only the EU and China have a hard approach, linked with enforceable and executable laws. It remains to be seen to what extent others will follow suit. A Brussels effect would also be desirable in this area, although there are already initial examples such as Brazil. A law regulating AI was approved there in December 2024. This law largely follows the EU AI Act.[15]

This multitude of political activities shows that politics has "woken up" and the mood has changed; the topic is now on the agenda. This follows a long period of unrestrained innovation without any regulation—the problems and potential dangers, alongside all achievements and positive possibilities, are too obvious. The crucial point will be whether it is possible to enforce effective governance models or regulations against the interests of the large platform companies. This could be further jeopardized by the political changes in the USA in January 2025. There, the new government seems to be more open to lobbying by the large platform companies, and they will use this opportunity to prevent or roll back regulations.[16] Are we heading toward a new feudal system of tech billionaires? This will be a central question for digital humanism.

It should also be critically noted that important points such as the military use are excluded—this will certainly make itself negatively noticeable in this phase of

---

[13] https://www.un.org/sites/un2.un.org/files/governing_ai_for_humanity_final_report_en.pdf.

[14] Such a capacity network should link up United Nations-affiliated capacity development centers, making available expertise and compute and AI training data to key actors (something like a distributed CERN).

[15] https://artificialintelligenceact.com/brazil-ai-act/.

[16] On his first day as president, Trump revoked an executive order issued by previous president Biden in 2023 that was intended to reduce the risks of AI. But he is not alone. In September 2024, the democratic governor of California vetoed an AI safety bill, even though polls showed a clear majority of the population in favor of the project. The tech industry, however, had massive objections.

geopolitical conflicts. In general, however, all these legal and regulatory proposals have a great proximity to digital humanism. The Digital Humanism Initiative has also been involved as a civil society initiative. In the long term, however, the sole focus on AI might be too short-sighted. Ultimately, it is about an ensemble of interconnected technologies; for me, AI is "just" another step in the never-ending wave of digitalization.

Technical Challenges

But we cannot only regulate the world, define guidelines, enact laws, and control, our goal as a society should also be the development and the deployment of trustworthy systems. They should be socially useful, enable the participation of the various interest groups, complement humans, and support their activities. At the same time, such an approach must address the problems of digital transformation described above and work toward eliminating them, for example, by making a system's decisions transparent, detecting and preventing malicious behavior, or ensuring the protection of personal data.

These goals formed the starting point for our workshop on the roadmap of digital humanism in March 2022, where the participants drafted and discussed the roadmap shown in Table 9.1 (Prem et al., 2022). On the horizontal axis, we find the dark sides of digitalization, as outlined in Chap. 6; on the vertical axis are the research questions and tasks, the answers to which contribute to solving the respective problems. Crosses in the cells indicate which research questions we consider essential for which critical issues.

Table 9.1 shows the full range of digital humanism and also the complexity of the task of designing a humane digital future.[17] It seems that almost everything is connected to everything else, which it largely is. I would like to show this with three examples of research issues from Table 9.1:

- *Fairness* is an important aspect in many problem areas, e.g.:
  - On the topic of AI and decision-making: How fair or biased are the training data?
  - In automation: Fairness is a crucial concept when considering the division of labor and the interaction between system and human.
  - On platforms: What would fair participation of users look like?
  - In online media: What is a fair distribution of interesting online content for which user group?
  - In the environmental question: Here, one often deals with economic considerations—what is a fair representation of the various interests in this context?

- *Explainability*: How can the decision proposed by a computer be explained, and why is such content or product suggested? This is an extremely difficult topic

---

[17] The table may also serve to define research and innovation programs of digital humanism.

Table 9.1 Digital Humanism—Research and Innovation Roadmap

Critical issues Research topics	AI and human control	Labor and automation	Surveillance	Platform and monopolies	Online media and fake news	Digital sovereignty	Environment and sustainability
Explainability	x	x			x		
Transparency	x		x		x		
Privacy	x		x			x	
Personalization	x		x	x	x		
Fairness	x	x		x	x		x
Norms and ethics	x	x	x	x	x	x	x
Accountability of systems and providers	x	x	x	x	x	x	x
Human/machine cooperation and control	x	x	x	x	x		
Participatory approaches	x	x			x		
Security			x			x	
regulatory approaches	x	x	x	x	x	x	x
Digital humanism business models		x	x	x	x	x	x
Content moderation	x		x		x		
Market mechanisms and power relations		x		x		x	
Resilience vs. efficiency (algorithms and architectures)	x	x		x		x	x
Open systems engineering (incl. interoperability, open data)			x	x		x	

Source: Prem et al. (2022). © Prem, Hardman, Werthner, Timmers

with the currently successful systems, which function as black boxes and have no explicit logic implemented. This is of importance when working with AI systems (AI and human control, in automation) and also in online media.
- *Efficiency* vs. *resilience*, with the latter also referring to fault-tolerant systems. Here, distributed architectures like the Internet and algorithms play a key role. This topic is essential in questions of automation, platforms, sovereignty, and the environment and fundamental for the organization of our economy and society.

However, this table is only a first step; it is not complete. It probably does not contain all relevant research topics, and more importantly, it does not list the various disciplines required for each of the research topics. Take, for example, the concept of fairness, for recommendation systems or search engines. How is fairness defined? Is it in relation to the provider of information or products, in relation to the readers or consumers, to which subgroups? Or how do we have to define fairness in relation to some general societal criteria? It is clear that in an interdisciplinary approach, disciplines such as sociology, political science, and economics are necessary and need to cooperate.

How the different topics are intertwined is also very well illustrated by the example of an online platform (Fig. 9.2), where in the upper bar, the respective services or activities of a platform are shown as a sequence, where one activity leads to the next or causes it. Starting with the digital hardware as the basis of the service platform, interaction data are logged and used for the creation of forecast models of human behavior, which in turn are used for digital marketing, which may ultimately lead to digital control by technology companies as new power centers (Prem, 2024).

In the lower bar of Fig. 9.2, the respective effects and subject areas of digital humanism are listed and how they are each linked to the respective services and activities of the platform. The complexity of this network of relationships and the mutual dependencies are striking. This also shows that digital humanism requires a holistic approach—both in the analysis of the impact and in the development of IT systems.

In the latter aspect—system development—the entire process must be considered, from analysis to design to the practical application. This poses a real challenge, as it is difficult, for example, to find a common language in which all participants use the same terms with identical meaning. Particularly challenging are the different perspectives and interests of the participants involved (Fig. 9.3; Sharp, 2024; Shneiderman, 2022). This raises several non-trivial questions: How do you integrate the different users of the system, especially since they are often unknown in the early stages? Who defines the system's objectives? Who determines how societal, often contradictory concerns are defined and implemented?[18] How can individual needs or those of the respective interest groups be reconciled with societal interests? How do you design communication and handling of change requests?

---

[18] Just take the design of a travel platform, especially a flight-booking platform. What objectives and criteria are used here, especially with regard to the environment? Perhaps no results should be provided here at all for environmental reasons.

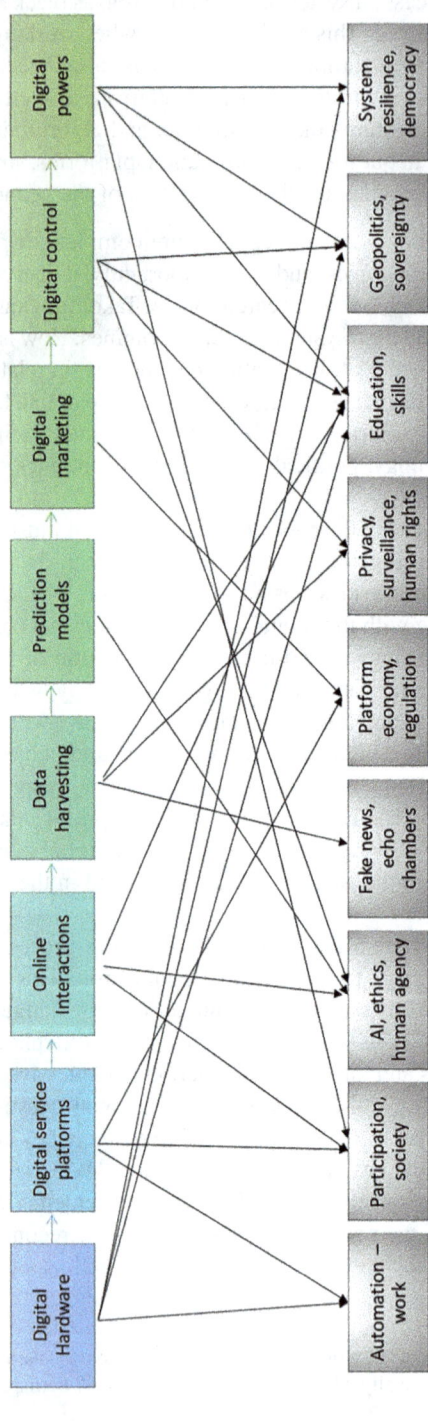

Fig. 9.2 A link between the development of digital technologies with central questions of digital humanism, using the example of social online networks. (Source: Prem, 2024. © Erich Prem)

Fig. 9.3 Design and development challenges in complex systems, taking human values into consideration. (After Shneiderman, 2022. © Hannes Werthner)

How do you effectively integrate the various participants, as shown in Fig. 9.3, into the process? And how do you address the threats mentioned? As you can see, apart from the not insignificant difficulties in defining the requirements and objectives of a system, the development itself poses also a major challenge.

This discussion also points at the critical issue of interdisciplinarity, especially in the academic field, both in research and in teaching. In research, the way the research landscape is organized in separate silos still hinders the necessary cooperation between disciplines. Especially young and interdisciplinary researchers often have serious problems obtaining funding and support. Their work requires knowledge in various fields, but they may not be sufficiently specialized in their core discipline. Interdisciplinarity carries the risk of knowing too little about too many things. And there is also the question of the extent to which the various disciplines are ready for this.

This seems to be true (at least to a large extent) for computer science, as it is playing a very active role in the current changes and is also aware of them. Other disciplines may not yet experience this so closely. However, "new" disciplines are already emerging at the interfaces, such as digital humanities or computational social science. And digital humanism can also be understood from this perspective. Interdisciplinarity concerns not only the tools and methods of research but also the change in the subject of research itself, especially when studying social constructs that are and will increasingly be shaped by technologies such as AI.[19]

And this breadth of disciplines also poses a challenge for teaching. There too, various disciplines need to be integrated without losing scientific depth. Computer science departments worldwide have begun to include topics such as ethics in their curricula, either as standalone courses or embedded in specific technical subjects.

---

[19] See also Milena Tsvetkova's blog (October 23, 2024), where she argues that social scientists should recognize and engage with the social properties of these new technologies. https://blogs.lse.ac.uk/impactofsocialsciences/2024/10/23/social-science-can-no-longer-ignore-the-social-actions-of-intelligent-machines/.

However, a truly broad interdisciplinary curriculum that covers the various aspects and disciplines is still lacking. But there are also positive developments, e.g., in system development with initial approaches to integrating ethical guidelines into the software process. Some companies already offer specific tools and associations like IEEE provide guidelines for the ethical design of systems (Spiekermann-Hoff, 2021; Neppel & Shaw, 2024; Zuber et al., 2024).

In general, one can see that digital humanism calls for a different technological path. Instead of focusing on pure automation and optimization, we should focus on resilience, sustainability, broad participation, and the enhancement of human capabilities. As already explained, such developments were already present in the early days of informatics, e.g., the work of Doug Engelbart with his fundamental research in the field of human-computer interaction and his Augmentation Research Center Lab at SRI International or that of Vannevar Bush with his Memex concept as a tool to supplement—not replace—humans. This tradition of human-centered technology is continued, for example, with the Human-in-the-Loop approach (Shneiderman, 2022; Sharp, 2024). In this context, the g0v community in Taiwan is also of interest. It explicitly promotes the transparency of government work and its communication, for example, with the development of information and participation platforms for citizens.[20]

Another promising approach to technology oriented toward the needs of humans, society, and nature is proposed by Siddarth et al. (2021), focusing on digital plurality. This rather general approach shows three interesting properties: it is complementary, i.e., it supplements and cooperates; it is participatory, i.e., it integrates and involves; and it is based on reciprocity, i.e., different approaches are pursued and integrated if possible. Whether such an approach will work and will be successful remains to be seen.

From what has been explained so far, it follows that digital humanism is not just about science and research. The concept of human-machine co-evolution also implies that technology does not develop on its own; it is determined by unequal societal and economic power relations. As I have explained, it is not just about technology; it also extends to politics. Digital humanism necessarily operates within a multidimensional framework with various levels:

- Different problem areas of digitalization, as described from platforms to sovereignty or work
- Different disciplines: informatics and technical/engineering disciplines, social science, and humanities; from analysis to system development, with the challenge of interdisciplinarity
- Different activities: applied and basic research, development and experiments, innovation, education, communication, and, finally, political intervention
- Various societal actors and stakeholders: from universities and schools, companies and interest groups, and public institutions to citizens and non-governmental organizations.

Digital Humanism is simple and at the same time complicated; it is a challenge (Neidhardt et al., 2022), but it has to be done.

---

[20] g0v.tw/intl/en/.

Chapter 10
Conclusion

In this book, I wanted to show the massive impact that technological development has, both positive and negative. Such an ambivalence of technological developments was already well described by John von Neuman in his essay "Can We Survive Technology" in relation to nuclear energy (von Neumann, 1955). Consequently, a description of digitalization cannot and must not be limited to technical aspects alone. It must be more comprehensive, and I hope that this has been achieved. Digital humanism is an almost-logical answer to this development. It is a response that analyzes and reflects but is also constructive, and it takes an interdisciplinary and ethical standpoint. In that sense, it is also optimistic; it assumes that we can interfere. Such an approach also touches on the political level, because technical, economic, and social change is ultimately a political question about power. Since there is no higher being responsible for these developments—and they do not follow any historical determinism—we, the people, should be the decisive force, not in an elitist way like the caste of the knowledgeable but following a democratic and participatory approach. Let us be disobedient and not obey—let us control and direct the process, especially since the development of IT will "not end," just like the changes enabled and triggered by IT. But this call for intervention does not only concern the digital world. This is especially true in the current times of political upheaval in a multi-polar world, with conflicts on a geopolitical level and where national egoism prevails. Developments in the IT sector also play a significant role. They do not make things any easier. This is another sign of the intertwining of the digital with the real.

We should not focus only on the optimal and fastest. We need a long-term and sustainable perspective. This is a lesson of digital humanism, which looks at the achievements, opportunities, and also dangers of technology and assumes that it can and must be designed and used for the benefit of a social and ecologically sustainable society. A statement of the Viennese Manifesto is that we must not only analyze and discuss but also act, both in scientific and practical terms. Let's do it!

Appendix: Vienna Manifesto on Digital Humanism, Vienna, May 2019

"The system is failing"—stated by the founder of the Web, Tim Berners-Lee—emphasizes that while digitalization opens unprecedented opportunities, it also raises serious concerns: the monopolization of the Web, the rise of extremist opinions and behavior orchestrated by social media, the formation of filter bubbles and echo chambers as islands of disjoint truths, the loss of privacy, and the spread of digital surveillance. Digital technologies are disrupting societies and questioning our understanding of what it means to be human. The stakes are high, and the challenge of building a just and democratic society with humans at the center of technological progress needs to be addressed with determination as well as scientific ingenuity. Technological innovation demands social innovation, and social innovation requires broad societal engagement.

This manifesto is a call to deliberate and to act on current and future technological development. We encourage our academic communities, as well as industrial leaders, politicians, policy makers, and professional societies all around the globe, to actively participate in policy formation. Our demands are the result of an emerging process that unites scientists and practitioners across fields and topics, brought together by concerns and hopes for the future. We are aware of our joint responsibility for the current situation and the future—both as professionals and citizens.

Today, we experience the co-evolution of technology and humankind. The flood of data, algorithms, and computational power is disrupting the very fabric of society by changing human interactions, societal institutions, economies, and political structures. Science and the humanities are not exempt. This disruption simultaneously creates and threatens jobs, produces and destroys wealth, and improves and damages our ecology. It shifts power structures, thereby blurring the human and the machine.

The quest is for enlightenment and humanism. The capability to automate human cognitive activities is a revolutionary aspect of computer science/informatics.

For many tasks, machines surpass already what humans can accomplish in speed, precision, and even analytic deduction. The time is right to bring together humanistic ideals with critical thoughts about technological progress. We therefore link this manifesto to the intellectual tradition of humanism and similar movements striving for an enlightened humanity.

Like all technologies, digital technologies do not emerge from nowhere. They are shaped by implicit and explicit choices and thus incorporate a set of values, norms, economic interests, and assumptions about how the world around us is or should be. Many of these choices remain hidden in software programs implementing algorithms that remain invisible. In line with the renowned Vienna Circle and its contributions to modern thinking, we want to espouse critical rational reasoning and the interdisciplinarity needed to shape the future.

We must shape technologies in accordance with human values and needs, instead of allowing technologies to shape humans. Our task is not only to rein in the downsides of information and communication technologies but also to encourage human-centered innovation. We call for a digital humanism that describes, analyzes, and, most importantly, influences the complex interplay of technology and humankind, for a better society and life, fully respecting universal human rights.

In conclusion, **we proclaim the following core principles**:

- **Digital technologies should be designed to promote democracy and inclusion**. This will require special efforts to overcome current inequalities and to use the emancipatory potential of digital technologies to make our societies more inclusive.
- **Privacy and freedom of speech are essential values for democracy and should be at the center of our activities.**
- **Effective regulations, rules, and laws, based on a broad public discourse, must be established**. They should ensure prediction accuracy, fairness and equality, accountability, and transparency of software programs and algorithms.
- **Regulators need to intervene with tech monopolies**. It is necessary to restore market competitiveness as tech monopolies concentrate market power and stifle innovation. Governments should not leave all decisions to markets.
- **Decisions with consequences that have the potential to affect individual or collective human rights must continue to be made by humans**. Decision-makers must be responsible and accountable for their decisions. Automated decision-making systems should only support human decision-making, not replace it.
- **Scientific approaches crossing different disciplines** are a prerequisite for tackling the challenges ahead. Technological disciplines such as computer science/informatics must collaborate with social sciences, humanities, and other sciences, breaking disciplinary silos.
- **Universities are the place where new knowledge is produced and critical thought is cultivated**. Hence, they have a special responsibility and have to be aware of that.

- **Academic and industrial researchers must engage openly with wider society and reflect upon their approaches.** This needs to be embedded in the practice of producing new knowledge and technologies while at the same time defending the freedom of thought and science.
- **Practitioners everywhere ought to acknowledge their shared responsibility for the impact of information technologies.** They need to understand that no technology is neutral and should be sensitized to see both potential benefits and possible downsides.
- **A vision is needed for new educational curricula, combining knowledge from the humanities, the social sciences, and engineering studies.** In the age of automated decision-making and AI, creativity and attention to human aspects are crucial to the education of future engineers and technologists.
- **Education on computer science/informatics and its societal impact must start as early as possible.** Students should learn to combine information-technology skills with awareness of the ethical and societal issues at stake.

We are at a crossroads to the future; we must go into action and take the right direction.

Bibliography

Acemoglu, D., & Autor, D. (2011). Skills, tasks and technologies: Implications for employment and earnings. *Handbook of Labor Economics, 4b*, 1043–1171.

Acemoglu, D., & Johnson, S. (2023). *Power and progress: Our 1000-year struggle for technology and prosperity*. Campus Verlag.

Acemoglu, D., & Restrepo, P. (2019). Automation and new tasks: How technology displaces and reinstates labor. *Journal of Economic Perspectives, 33*(2), 3–30.

Acemoglu, D., Robinson, J. (2023): Weak, Despotic, or Inclusive? How State Type Emerges from State versus Civil Society Competition. American Political Science Review (2023) 117, 2, 407–420

Aggarwal, C. (2023). *Neural networks and deep learning. A textbook* (2nd ed.). Springer.

Ahmed, N., Wahed, M., Thompson, N. (2023): The growing influence of industry in AI research. Science, 379 (6635).

Autor, D. H. (2014). Skills, education, and the rise of earnings inequality among the "Other 99 Percent". *Science, 344*, 6186.

Baeza Yates, R., & Fayyad, U. (2022). The attention economy and the impact of artificial intelligence. In H. Werthner, E. Prem, A. Lee, & C. Ghezzi (Eds.), *Perspectives on digital humanism*. Springer.

Baeza-Yates, R., & Murgai, L. (2024). Bias and the web. In H. Werthner, C. Ghezzi, J. Kramer, J. Nida-Rümelin, B. Nuseibeh, E. Prem, & A. Stanger (Eds.), *Introduction to digital humanism. A textbook*. Springer.

Bell, D. (1976). *The cultural contradictions of capitalism*. Basic Books.

Bennaceur, A., Ghezzi, C., Kramer, J., & Nuseibeh, B. (2024). Responsible software engineering: Requirements and goals. In H. Werthner, C. Ghezzi, J. Kramer, J. Nida-Rümelin, B. Nuseibeh, E. Prem, & A. Stanger (Eds.), *Introduction to digital humanism. A textbook*. Springer.

Bradford, A. (2019). *The Brussels effect: How the European Union rules the world*. Oxford University Press.

Brynjolfsson, E. (1993). The productivity paradox of information technology. *CACM, 36*(12), 66–77.

Brynjolfsson, E., & Hitt, L. (1996). Paradox lost? Firm-level evidence on the returns to information systems spending. *Management Science, 42*(4), 541–558.

Brynjolfsson, E., Li, D., & Raymond, L. (2023). *Generative AI at work*. NBER Working Paper No. w31161.

Campitelli, G., & Gobet, F. (2010). Herbert Simon's decision-making approach: Investigation of cognitive processes in experts. *Review of General Psychology, 14*(4), 354–364.

Cano, A. (2018). A survey on graphic processing unit computing for large-scale data mining. *Wiley Interdisciplinary Reviews: Data Mining and Knowledge Discovery, 8*(1), e1232.

Cho, Y. (2023). *Common sense: The dark matter of language and intelligence.* VLDB 2023 Keynote.

Clark, C. (2023). *Spring of the revolution.* DVA.

Codagnone, C. (2023, November). *Online platform: Power, regulation, and the transatlantic relationship. Can machines save the world? Digital Humanism Conference Vienna.* Retrieved from https://caiml.org/machines2023/program/cristiano-codagnone-slides.pdf

Cortada, J., & Aspray, W. (2019). *Fake News nation: The long history of lies and misinterpretations in America.* Rowman & Littlefield.

Crawford, K. (2021). *Atlas of AI: Power, politics, and the planetary costs of artificial intelligence.* Yale University Press.

Cusumano, M. (2023). Generative AI as a new innovation platform. *CACM, 66*(10), 18–21.

Danziger, S., Levav, J., & Avnaim-Pesso, L. (2011). Extraneous factors in judicial decisions. *Proceedings of the National Academy of Sciences of the USA, 108*(17), 6889–6892.

Dolata, U., & Schrape, J. F. (2023). Platform companies on the internet as a new organizational form. A sociological perspective. *Innovation: The European Journal of Social Science Research,* 1–20.

Doueihi, M. (2011). *For a digital humanism.* Editions Seuil.

Drucker, P. (1969). *The age of discontinuity: Guidelines to our changing society.* Harper & Row.

Eichinger, A., Knees, P., & Werthner, H. (2024). *Digitalisierung und Wir (in German).* Residenzverlag.

Farrell, H., & Newman, A. (2019). Weaponized interdependence: How global economic networks shape state coercion. *International Security, 44*(1), 42–79.

Farrell, H., & Newman, A. (2023). *Underground empire: How America weaponized the world economy.* Penguin Books.

Friedman, T. (2005). *The world is flat: A brief history of the twenty-first century.* Farrar, Straus and Giroux.

Fukuyama, F. (1992). *The end of history and the last man.* Free Press.

Gawer, A. (2022). Digital platforms and ecosystems: Remarks on the dominant organizational forms of the digital age. *Innovations, 24*(1), 110–124.

Gmyrek, P., Berg, J., & Bescond, D. (2023, August). *Generative AI and jobs: A global analysis of potential effects on job quantity and quality.* ILO Working Paper 96.

Gurbaxani, V., & Whang, S. (1991). The impact of information systems on organizations and markets. *Communications of the ACM, 34*(1), 59–73.

Haigh, T. (2024). Historical reflections: How the AI boom went bust. *CACM, 67*(2), 22.

Haigh, T., & Ceruzzi, P. (2021). *A new history of modern computing.* MIT Press.

Hanson, R. (1998). *Long term growth as a sequence of exponential modes.* Retrieved from http://hanson.berkeley.edu/longgrow.html

Hardin, G. (1968). The tragedy of the commons. *Science, 162,* 1243–1248.

Hey, T., Tansley, S., Tolle, K., & Gray, J. (Eds.). (2009). *The Fourth Paradigm: Data-intensive scientific discovery.* Microsoft Research.

Hodges, A. (1989). *Alan Turing—Enigma.* (R. Herken & E. Lack, Trans.). Kammerer and Unverzagt.

Humlum, A., & Vestergaard, E. (2024). *The adoption of ChatGPT.* IZA Discussion Paper, 16992.

Isaacson, W. (2011). *Steve Jobs.* Simon & Schuster.

John Hughes, J. et al., (2024). Best-of-N Jailbreaking. arXiv preprint arXiv:2412.03556v2.

Kahneman, D. (2011). *Thinking, fast and slow.* Farrar, Straus and Giroux.

Krause, G. (2023). *The practice of digital humanism. What contribution companies can make and how they can benefit from it.* Springer.

Kurzweil, R. (2005). *The singularity is near: When humans transcend biology.* Dewey Decimal.

Larus, J. (2024). Evolution of computing. In H. Werthner, C. Ghezzi, J. Kramer, J. Nida-Rümelin, B. Nuseibeh, E. Prem, & A. Stanger (Eds.), *Introduction to digital humanism. A textbook.* Springer.

Larus, J., Hankin, C., Carson, S. G., Christen, M., Crafa, S., Grau, O., Kirchner, C., Knowles, B., McGettrick, V., Tamburri, D. A., & Werthner, H. (2018). *When computers decide: European recommendations on machine-learned automated decision making*. Joint report Informatics Europe & EUACM. Retrieved from www.informatics-europe.org/publications

Lee, E. (2020). *The coevolution. The entwined futures of humans and machines*. MIT Press.

Lee, E. (2022). Are we losing control? In H. Werthner, E. Prem, A. Lee, & C. Ghezzi (Eds.), *Perspectives on digital humanism*. Springer.

Lindorfer, M. (2024). The threat of surveillance and the need for privacy protections. In H. Werthner, C. Ghezzi, J. Kramer, J. Nida-Rümelin, B. Nuseibeh, E. Prem, & A. Stanger (Eds.), *Introduction to digital humanism. A textbook*. Springer.

Maslej, N., Fattorini, L., Perrault, R., Parli, V., Reuel, A., Brynjolfsson, E., Etchemendy, J., Ligett, K., Lyons, T., Manyika, J., Niebles, J. C., Shoham, Y., Wald, R., & Clark, J. (2024). *The AI index 2024 annual report*. AI Index Steering Committee, Institute for Human-Centered AI, Stanford University.

McCulloch, W., & Pitts, W. (1943). A logical calculus of the ideas immanent in nervous activity. *Bulletin of Mathematical Biophysics, 5*, 115–133.

Metakides, G. (2024). Democracy in the digital era. In H. Werthner, C. Ghezzi, J. Kramer, J. Nida-Rümelin, B. Nuseibeh, E. Prem, & A. Stanger (Eds.), *Introduction to digital humanism. A textbook*. Springer.

Müller, M., & Kettemann, M. (2024). European approaches to the regulation of digital technologies. In H. Werthner, C. Ghezzi, J. Kramer, J. Nida-Rümelin, B. Nuseibeh, E. Prem, & A. Stanger (Eds.), *Introduction to digital humanism. A textbook*. Springer.

Munn, L. (2024). Digital labor, platforms, and AI. In H. Werthner, C. Ghezzi, J. Kramer, J. Nida-Rümelin, B. Nuseibeh, E. Prem, & A. Stanger (Eds.), *Introduction to digital humanism. A textbook*. Springer.

Neidhardt, J., Werthner, H., & Woltran, S. (2022). It is simple, it is complicated. In H. Werthner, E. Prem, A. Lee, & C. Ghezzi (Eds.), *Perspectives on digital humanism*. Springer.

Neppel, C., & Shaw, P. (2024). Governance for digital humanism: The role of regulation, standardization, and certification. In H. Werthner, C. Ghezzi, J. Kramer, J. Nida-Rümelin, B. Nuseibeh, E. Prem, & A. Stanger (Eds.), *Introduction to digital humanism. A textbook*. Springer.

Nida-Rümelin, J., & Staudacher, K. (2024). Philosophical foundations of digital humanism. In H. Werthner, C. Ghezzi, J. Kramer, J. Nida-Rümelin, B. Nuseibeh, E. Prem, & A. Stanger (Eds.), *Introduction to digital humanism. A textbook*. Springer.

Nida-Rümelin, J., & Weidenfeld, N. (2018). *Digital humanism*. Piper.

Nida-Rümelin, J., & Winter, D. (2024). Humanism and enlightenment. In H. Werthner, C. Ghezzi, J. Kramer, J. Nida-Rümelin, B. Nuseibeh, E. Prem, & A. Stanger (Eds.), *Introduction to digital humanism. A textbook*. Springer.

Noy, S., & Zhang, W. (2023). Experimental evidence on the productivity effects of generative artificial intelligence. *Science, 381*(6654), 187–192.

Nygaard, K. (1986). Program development as a social activity. In H. J. Kugler (Ed.), *Information processing 86, Elsevier Science, IFIP. Proceedings from the IFIP 10th World Computer Congress, Dublin, Ireland*.

O'Regan, G. (2021). *A brief history of computing*. Springer.

Ostrom, E. (1990). *Governing the commons: The evolution of institutions for collective action*. Cambridge University Press.

Parker, G., & Van Alstyne, M. (2024). Platforms: Their structure, benefits, and challenges. In H. Werthner, C. Ghezzi, J. Kramer, J. Nida-Rümelin, B. Nuseibeh, E. Prem, & A. Stanger (Eds.), *Introduction to digital humanism. A textbook*. Springer.

Parker, G. G., Van Alstyne, M. W., & Choudary, S. P. (2016). *Platform revolution: How networked markets are transforming the economy and how to make them work for you*. WW Norton & Company.

Peng, S., Kalliamvakou, E., Cihon, P., & Demirer, M. (2023). The impact of AI on developer productivity: Evidence from GitHub copilot. arXiv preprint arXiv:2302.06590.

Perez, C. (2002). *Technological revolutions and financial capital: The dynamics of bubbles and golden ages*. Elgar.

Peterson, T. L., Ferreira, R., & Vardi, M. Y. (2023). *Abstracted power and responsibility in computer science ethics education*. IEEE Transactions on Technology and Society.

Piketty, T. (2021): Time for Socialism - Dispatches from a World on Fire, 2016-2021. Yale University Press.

Popper, K. (1969). Moral responsibility of the scientist. *Encounters, 2*(3), 279–283.

Porter, M. E. (1980). *Competitive strategy*. Free Press.

Prem, E. (2024). Principles of digital humanism: A critical post-humanist view. *Journal of Responsible Technology, 17*, 100075.

Prem, E., & Krenn, B. (2024). On algorithmic content moderation. In H. Werthner, C. Ghezzi, J. Kramer, J. Nida-Rümelin, B. Nuseibeh, E. Prem, & A. Stanger (Eds.), *Introduction to digital humanism. A textbook*. Springer.

Prem, E., Hardman, L., Werthner, H., & Timmers, P. (Eds.). (2022). *Research, innovation and education roadmap for digital humanism*. The Digital Humanism Initiative. Retrieved from owncloud.tuwien.ac.at/index.php/s/vmZSxsuruhk77Iy

Reichl, P. (2024). *Homo cyber*. Müry Salzmann Verlag.

Rotenberg, M. (2024). Human rights alignment: The challenge ahead for AI lawmakers. In H. Werthner, C. Ghezzi, J. Kramer, J. Nida-Rümelin, B. Nuseibeh, E. Prem, & A. Stanger (Eds.), *Introduction to digital humanism. A textbook*. Springer.

Samaan, D. (2024). Work in a new world. In H. Werthner, C. Ghezzi, J. Kramer, J. Nida-Rümelin, B. Nuseibeh, E. Prem, & A. Stanger (Eds.), *Introduction to digital humanism. A textbook*. Springer.

Schmidhuber, J. (2015). Deep learning in neural networks: An overview. *Neural Networks, 61*, 85–117.

Searle, J. (1980). Minds, brains, and programs. *The Behavioral and Brain Sciences, 3*, 417–457.

Sigmund, K. (2017): Exact Thinking in Demented Times: The Vienna Circle and the Epic Quest for the Foundations of Science. Basic Books.

Sharp, H. (2024). Humans in the loop: People at the heart of systems development. In H. Werthner, C. Ghezzi, J. Kramer, J. Nida-Rümelin, B. Nuseibeh, E. Prem, & A. Stanger (Eds.), *Introduction to digital humanism. A textbook*. Springer.

Shneiderman, B. (2022). *Human-centered AI*. Oxford University Press.

Shumailov, I., Shumaylov, Z., Zhao, Y., et al. (2024). AI models collapse when trained on recursively generated data. *Nature, 631*, 755–759. https://doi.org/10.1038/s41586-024-07566-y

Siddarth, D., Acemoglu, D., Allen, D., Crawford, K., Evans, J., & Jordan, M. (2021). *How AI fails us*. Technology & Democracy Discussion Paper. Harvard University.

Simon, H. (1976). *Administrative behavior* (3rd ed.). The Free Press.

Spiekermann-Hoff, S. (2021). What to expect from IEEE 7000TM. The first standard for building ethical systems. *IEEE Technology and Society Magazine, 40*(3), 99–100.

Stanger, A. (2020). Consumers vs. citizens in democracy's public sphere. *CACM, 63*(7), 29–31.

Strassnig, M., Mayer, K., Stampfer, M., & Zingerle, S. (2019). *Actors, instruments and topics for a digital humanism initiative in Vienna*. Study WWTF on behalf of the City of Vienna.

Timmers, P. (2024). Sovereignty in the digital age. In H. Werthner, C. Ghezzi, J. Kramer, J. Nida-Rümelin, B. Nuseibeh, E. Prem, & A. Stanger (Eds.), *Introduction to digital humanism. A textbook*. Springer.

Tubaro, P., Casilli, A. A., & Coville, M. (2020). The trainer, the verifier, the imitator: Three ways in which human platform workers support artificial intelligence. *Big Data & Society, 7*(1).

Turing, A. (1936). On computable numbers, with an application to the decision problem. *Proceedings of the London Mathematical Society, 58*, 230–265.

Turing, A. M. (1950). Computing machinery and intelligence. *Mind, 59*, 433–460.

Vardi, M. (2018). How the hippies destroyed the Internet. *CACM, 61*(7), 9.

Vardi, M. (2024a). Computing, you have blood on your hands! *CACM, 67*(1), 5.

Vardi, M. (2024b). Resilience: The key to planetary and societal sustainability. In H. Werthner, C. Ghezzi, J. Kramer, J. Nida-Rümelin, B. Nuseibeh, E. Prem, & A. Stanger (Eds.), *Introduction to digital humanism. A textbook*. Springer.

Vaswani, A., Shazeer, N., Parmar, N., Uszkoreit, J., Jones, L., Gomez, A., Kaiser, Ł., & Polosukhin, I. (2017). Attention is all you need. NIPS'17: Proceedings of the 31st International Conference on Neural Information Processing Systems. In N. Vincent & B. Hecht (Eds.), *A deeper investigation of the importance of Wikipedia links to search engine results. Proceedings of the ACM on Human-Computer Interaction 5 (CSCW1)* (pp. 1–15).

Vincent, N., Hecht, B. (2021): A Deeper Investigation of the Importance of Wikipedia Links to Search Engine Results. Proceedings of the ACM on Human-Computer Interaction 5 (CSCW1): 1–15.

von Neumann, J. (1955). In A. Taub (Ed.), *Collected works* (Vol. VI). A. Pergamon Press.

Warnke, M., & Woesler, M. (2024). *Sozialkybernetik in statu nascendi—Die Entstehungsgeschichte des chinesischen Sozialkredit-Systems (in German)*. Matthes & Seitz.

Weiser, M. (1991). The computer for the 21st century. *Scientific American, 265*, 94–105.

Weizenbaum, J. (1966). ELIZA—A computer program for the study of natural language communication between man and machine. *Communications of the ACM, 9*(1), 36–45.

Weizenbaum, J. (1976). *Computer power and human reason: From judgment to calculation*. W. H. Freeman & Co.

Werthner, H. (2020). The Viennese manifesto for digital humanism. In M. Hengstschläger (Ed.), *Digital change and ethics*. Ecowin Publishing.

Werthner, H. (2022a). From absolute nonsense to the world's operating system. *Electronic Markets, 32*, 145–151.

Werthner, H. (2022b). Geopolitics, digital sovereignty ... What's in a word? In H. Werthner, E. Prem, A. Lee, & C. Ghezzi (Eds.), *Perspectives on digital humanism*. Springer.

Werthner, H. (2024). Digital transformation, digital humanism: What needs to be done. In H. Werthner, C. Ghezzi, J. Kramer, J. Nida-Rümelin, B. Nuseibeh, E. Prem, & A. Stanger (Eds.), *Introduction to digital humanism. A textbook*. Springer.

Werthner, H. (2025). *Digitaler Humanismus. Über Digitalisierung und Künstliche Intelligenz (in German)*. Picus Verlag.

Werthner, H., Prem, E., Lee, A., & Ghezzi, C. (2022a). Preface. In H. Werthner, E. Prem, A. Lee, & C. Ghezzi (Eds.), *Perspectives on digital humanism*. Springer.

Werthner, H., Prem, E., Lee, A., & Ghezzi, C. (Eds.). (2022b). *Perspectives on digital humanism*. Springer.

Werthner, H., Stanger, A., Schiaffonati, V., Knees, P., Hardman, L., & Ghezzi, C. (2023). Digital humanism: The time is now. *IEEE Computer, 56*(1), 138–142.

Werthner, H., Ghezzi, C., Kramer, J., Nida-Rümelin, J., Nuseibeh, B., Prem, E., & Stanger, A. (2024). *Introduction to digital humanism. A textbook*. Springer.

Wiener, N. (1948). *Cybernetics or control and communication in the animal and the machine*. MIT Press.

Wigand, R. (1995). Electronic commerce reduced transaction costs. *Electronic Markets, 5*(3), 1–5.

Williamson, O. (1985). *The economic institutions of capitalism*. Macmillan.

Wing, J. M. (2006). Computational thinking. *Communications of the ACM, 49*, 33–35.

Zhang, A. (2024). *High wire: How China regulates big tech and governs its economy*. Oxford University Press.

Žižek, S. (2009). *First as tragedy, then as farce* (pp. 131–132). Verso Books.

Zuber, N., Gogoll, J., Kacianka, S., Nida-Rümelin, J., & Pretschner, A. (2024). Value-sensitive software design: Ethical deliberation in agile development processes. In H. Werthner, C. Ghezzi, J. Kramer, J. Nida-Rümelin, B. Nuseibeh, E. Prem, & A. Stanger (Eds.), *Introduction to digital humanism. A textbook*. Springer.

Zuboff, S. (2019). *The age of surveillance capitalism. The fight for a human future at the New Frontier of power*. Public Affairs.

GPSR Compliance
The European Union's (EU) General Product Safety Regulation (GPSR) is a set of rules that requires consumer products to be safe and our obligations to ensure this.

If you have any concerns about our products, you can contact us on

ProductSafety@springernature.com

In case Publisher is established outside the EU, the EU authorized representative is:

Springer Nature Customer Service Center GmbH
Europaplatz 3
69115 Heidelberg, Germany